Literature-Based
Reading Activities

Literature-Based Reading Activities

FOURTH EDITION

Hallie Kay Yopp
California State University, Fullerton

Ruth Helen Yopp
California State University, Fullerton

PEARSON

Boston   New York   San Francisco
Mexico City   Montreal   Toronto   London   Madrid   Munich   Paris
Hong Kong   Singapore   Tokyo   Cape Town   Sydney

Senior Series Editor: Aurora Martínez Ramos
Series Editorial Assistant: Kevin Shannon
Senior Marketing Manager: Krista Groshong
Production Editor: Annette Joseph
Editorial Production Service: Lynda Griffiths
Composition Buyer: Linda Cox
Manufacturing Buyer: Andrew Turso
Electronic Composition: Publishers' Design and Production Services, Inc.
Cover Administrator: Linda Knowles

For related titles and support materials, visit our online catalog at
www.ablongman.com.

Between the time website information is gathered and then published, it is not
unusual for some sites to have closed. Also, the transcription of URLs can result
in typographical errors. The publisher would appreciate notification where these
errors occur so that they may be corrected in subsequent editions.

ISBN 0-205-44248-X

Printed in the United States of America

10 9 8 7 6 5   09 08 07

Contents

Preface

Literature can be a powerful force in the lives of human beings. It can make us feel, think, and wonder. It can provide us with exciting, interesting information and new ways of looking at the world. It can change who we are forever.

Literature-Based Reading Activities is based on the beliefs that quality literature is an essential component of classroom activity and learning and that teachers should engage their students in thinking deeply about ideas in literature, making connections with literature, and responding to literature in ways that enrich their lives. It is also based on the beliefs that students bring unique perspectives, experiences, and contexts to their reading of literature and that social interaction is at the heart of learning. Thus, in this book we share activities that are intended to inspire students to bring themselves to the literature, engage with ideas in books, and expand their understandings and responses through interactions with peers.

Since we wrote the first edition of this book in the early 1990s, our children have grown from infants and toddlers to adolescents. In that time, they have enjoyed many great books at home and at school, and we are reminded almost daily of how important literature—and you, their teachers—are in the lives of children. You influence them every day with the decisions you make—decisions to share good books, decisions to provide meaningful experiences, and decisions to listen. We have been fortunate indeed to have had our children in classrooms where teachers provide thought-provoking experiences with literature that respect and value students.

In this fourth edition, we update chapters by incorporating current research, more thoroughly address issues related to teaching children whose first language is not English, provide more than a dozen new activities, and offer many new examples.

The organization of the book remains the same as in previous editions. Chapter One provides important background information, including the rationale for using literature in the classroom, the influence of three theoretical perspectives on classroom practice, a discussion of teachers' responsibilities when using literature, and the criteria we used in selecting activities to include in this book. Chapters Two, Three, and Four provide descriptions of pre-, during, and postreading activities for literature-based reading experiences, along with examples of their application at several grade levels. Examples are shared for a variety of genres, including folktales, fantasy, realistic fiction, historical fiction, poetry, biography, and informational books. Because one of the most exciting ways to extend the literature experience is for students to create their own books, Chapter Five is devoted to the construction of individual and class books. A few important final comments are offered in the Afterword. Lists of websites that provide information about children's literature and titles of award-winning books are included in the appendices.

We wish to acknowledge the following reviewers who provided helpful comments about the book: Leena S. Furtado, California State University, Dominguez Hill; Avril Moore, Fontbonne University; Evelyn Priddy, Huntington College; and Jennifer Moon Ro, Binghamton University–SUNY.

We are grateful to the following people for their contributions to this book: Nancy Brewbaker, Paula Gray, and Alan Saldivar, Example 3.26; Doreen Fernandez, Janie Frigge, Kimberly Hennessy, and Thursa Williams, Example 4.6; and Jeanine Rossi, retelling picture book example.

We also thank Aurora Martinez, our editor at Allyn and Bacon, for her vision and support of this project; Kevin Shannon, our editorial assistant, for his attention to this fourth edition; and Lynda Griffiths for her careful editing.

Finally, we thank our husbands, Bert Slowik and Tom Edwards, and our children, Peter, Erica, Billy, and Dan, for their love and support.

CHAPTER ONE

Using Literature in the Classroom _____

LITERATURE IN THE CLASSROOM

Literature plays an important role in the lives and learning of students in many classrooms. In these classrooms, teachers read aloud good stories and interesting informational books, they provide regular independent reading time along with rich classroom libraries, they structure opportunities for students to share their responses to books with one another, and they explore works of literature with their students as part of the instructional program. Some teachers implement a literature-based reading program in which high-quality literature serves as the basis of reading instruction, and others supplement published reading programs with works of literature or integrate literature into other areas of the curriculum. The fortunate students of all these teachers benefit in many ways from the literature-rich experiences and environments their teachers provide; chief among these is that they experience the joy and satisfaction of reading.

Research has shown that the use of literature supports many aspects of literacy development (Galda & Cullinan, 2003). Literature facilitates language development in both younger and older students (Chomsky, 1972; Morrow, 1992; Nagy, Herman, & Anderson, 1985). It increases reading comprehension (Cohen, 1968; DeFord, 1981; Feitelson, Kita, & Goldstein, 1986; Morrow, 1992; Morrow, O'Connor, & Smith, 1990). It positively influences students' perceptions of and attitudes toward reading (Eldredge & Butterfield, 1986; Hagerty, Hiebert, & Owens, 1989; Larrick, 1987; Morrow, 1992; Tunnell & Jacobs, 1989). Literature influences writing ability (DeFord, 1981, 1984; Eckhoff, 1983; Lancia, 1997) and deepens knowledge of written language and written linguistic features (Purcell-Gates, McIntyre, & Freppon, 1995). Further, it has been suggested that the use of literature in the content areas (such as social studies and science) results in greater student understanding of and engagement with the content (Bean, 2000; Morrow & Gambrell, 2000).

When we examine what we believe are the goals of literacy instruction—to develop students' ability to learn with text; to expand their ability to think broadly, deeply, and critically about ideas in text; to promote personal responses to text; to nurture a desire to read; and to develop lifelong learners who can use text information to satisfy personal needs and interests and fully and wisely participate in society—the value of literature becomes obvious. How are teachers to stimulate minds and hearts without good literature? How are students to explore ideas, come to understand the perspectives of others, grow in their thinking, and develop a love of reading without good literature? Literature nurtures the imagination, provides enjoyment, and supports the understanding of ourselves, others, and the world in which we live. Without authentic and compelling texts and meaningful instructional contexts, quality literacy instruction cannot happen (Raphael, 2000) and we cannot achieve the goals that we hold dear.

Today's literature-based instruction is influenced by three theoretical perspectives: reader response, cognitive-constructivist, and sociocultural. Reader-response theories, which had their beginnings with I. A. Richards (1929) and Louise Rosenblatt (1938). Prior to the work of Richards and Rosenblatt, literary theory focused primarily on the author and then on the text and largely ignored the role of the reader. Reader-response theories emphasized that what the reader brings to the reading process matters just as what the author brings to the process matters and that, without a reader, texts are merely marks on a page. The reader's experiences, feelings, beliefs, attitudes, and knowledge all influence his or her reading of a text and are, in turn, influenced by the text.

Authorities identify several groups of reader-response theorists, but it is Rosenblatt who ultimately had the greatest influence on teachers, although it was not until the 1970s and 1980s that her ideas gained a wide audience. In Rosenblatt's view, a transaction between the reader and the text occurs during the reading process. The transaction is influenced, in part, by the stance that a reader assumes during reading. The reader can take a predominantly aesthetic stance or a predominantly efferent stance. When taking an *aesthetic* stance, the reader focuses on feeling states during the reading, the lived-through experience of the reading. Emotions, associations, ideas, and attitudes are aroused in the reader during an aesthetic stance. You probably take a predominantly aesthetic stance when reading a mystery novel—you are curious about who committed the crime, you worry about the safety of the hero or heroine with whom you may be identifying, your heart beats a little faster at the climax, and you are relieved when the mystery is solved. In contrast, an *efferent* stance is one in which the reader attends to information that he or she wishes to acquire from the text for some reason, either self-imposed or imposed by others. You likely take a predominantly efferent stance when reading directions for setting up a new gadget in your home. Your purpose is to gather data so that you can make all the right connections and have a fully operational piece of equipment at your disposal.

It should not be assumed, however, that efferent reading happens only with informational text and that aesthetic reading occurs only with fictional text. Have you ever experienced confusion about a character in a book and flipped back through the pages to remind yourself just exactly what his relationship is with the protagonist? You were engaging in efferent reading. Your purpose was to gather information and to ensure you knew the character's identity. Conversely, have you responded to an informational text by recalling experiences and feelings related to the topic? Have you ever had a visceral reaction to the content of informational text? If so, you were reading aesthetically.

A reader's stance falls along a continuum from aesthetic to efferent and changes from text to text, situation to situation, and moment to moment. It is influenced by many factors, including the text, the reader, the context, and—in the case of students—the teacher. When teachers focus on the information in texts, they promote an efferent stance: students read to gather and remember information. When teachers encourage enjoyment of the reading experience and invite and accept personal responses to the reading; when they ask students to recapture the lived-through experience of the reading through drawing, dancing, talking, writing, or role playing; when they allow students to build, express, and support their own interpretations of the text, they promote an aesthetic stance. Unfortunately, teachers often use activities with their students that evoke only efferent responses (Beach, 1993). Although gaining information from texts is important, reader-response theorists argue that students should also have many opportunities to respond aesthetically to literature.

Teachers who are influenced by reader-response theories understand that readers bring different backgrounds, experiences, understandings, and attitudes to their reading. These educators believe that reading is an experience accompanied by feelings and meanings and that responses resulting from a transaction between the reader and the text are dependent, in part, on the stance a reader takes and the opportunities for response that teachers provide. They foster students' aesthetic responses to literature. They respect different interpretations of text, rejecting the notion of one correct response, and they support students in reflecting on and revising their interpretations by prompting them to revisit the text and discuss their ideas with peers.

Like reader-response theories, cognitive-constructivist views of learning emphasize the importance of the reader in the reading process (Graves, Juel, & Graves, 2004) and inform classroom practice. According to cognitive-constructive views, readers are not empty vessels or *tabula rasas* but, rather, bring complex networks of knowledge and experiences with them to a text. They use their knowledge and experiences as they construct understandings of a reading selection, and because different readers bring different backgrounds, experiences, and purposes to their reading, no two readers construct exactly the same understandings. Cognitive-constructive theorists emphasize the active nature of reading. Meaning making is the result of cognitive work, with more complex or unfamiliar texts requiring more work if understandings are to be constructed. Teachers who are influenced by cognitive-constructivist views of reading provide time and opportunities for students to think about what they already know and to extend their knowledge networks in a variety of ways, including learning from those around them. They appreciate the subjectivity of the reading experience. They engage their students in activities that require them to actively process the text, for example, by considering ideas, organizing information, and making links among ideas in books and with their own lives.

The third group of theories relevant to the rich use of literature in the classroom are sociocultural theories, which emphasize the social nature of learning. Based on the work of Vygotsky (1978), who asserted that children learn through language-based social interactions, sociocultural theorists believe that learning is fundamentally a social process and that interactions among learners are crucial. These notions are clearly germane to students' interactions with text. In fact, many reading researchers maintain that deep-level understanding of text occurs only through interactions with others (Morrow & Gambrell, 2000). Teachers who understand that it is through language exchanges that students organize thought and construct meanings provide many opportunities for students to work together. They structure their classroom environments and learning experiences to promote student interactions. They ensure that students engage in discussions and negotiate their evolving understandings and interpretations of text with peers.

A mainstay of learning in a sociocultural perspective, discussion, can take several forms. Traditionally, classroom discussions have been highly centralized—the teacher decides what the students will talk about and facilitates the discussion. A more decentralized view of discussion—one that deemphasizes the role of the teacher—has been advocated by many educators in the past decade (Almasi, 1995, 1996; Jewell & Pratt, 1999; Langer, 1995; Wiencek & O'Flahavan, 1994). In this view, discussions are led by students and guided by their responses to a book. Small student-led group discussions provide students with opportunities to attain social and interpretive authority and may increase participation from students who are reluctant to speak in teacher-directed situations (Raphael, 2000). Unfortunately, although widely promoted in the professional literature, peer-led discussions are rare in classrooms (Almasi, O'Flahavan, & Ayra, 2001).

Computer-mediated discussions are a recent alternative to teacher-led and student-led discussions. In these on-line discussions, students build their understandings of and share their responses to books with students from other schools, states, and even countries. These discussions provide all students with the opportunity to respond to the comments of peers and may allow students who feel marginalized to more fully participate in a discussion (Gambrell, 2004). All three forms of discussion—teacher-led, student-led, and computer-mediated—have a place in the classroom, and the value of each depends on the particular and varying goals for discussion.

The purpose of this book is to assist teachers in providing their students with meaningful experiences with literature. We offer a variety of activities that are rooted in reader response, cognitive-constructive, and sociocultural perspectives. The activities honor the readers by acknowledging that their backgrounds, knowledge, and experiences influence their transactions with literature and by inviting them to respond both efferently and aesthetically. Additionally, the activities honor the active engagement required for meaning making by prompting thoughtful interactions with text. Also, they honor the crucial role of social interaction in the construction of meaning as they stimulate discussion and collaboration.

In the next section, we describe key responsibilities of teachers as they share literature with their students. Then, we identify questions that guided our thinking as we selected activities to include in this book.

TEACHER RESPONSIBILITIES

1. *Know children's literature.* Familiarize yourself with a wide variety of children's literature, and keep abreast of newly published works. Spend time in libraries and bookstores. Browse websites that provide lists of award-winning literature, reviews of children's literature, and ideas for using literature. (Some of these websites are listed in Appendix A, and recipients of several major awards are listed in Appendix B.) Talk to colleagues about books and consider establishing book clubs at your school site. It is difficult to share great literature with students unless you are familiar with it yourself.

2. *Provide students with access to a wide variety of children's literature.* Develop a rich classroom library that includes selections reflecting a wide range of interests, topics, and difficulty levels. Make available a variety of genres, including informational books, which are a scarcity in many classrooms (Duke, 1999; Yopp & Yopp, 1999). Research has revealed that the availability of reading materials in extensive classroom libraries and opportunities to choose books are key factors in motivating students to read (Guthrie & Wigfield, 2000; Palmer, Codling, & Gambrell, 1994; Worthy, 2000, 2002).

3. *Provide time for reading and talking about books.* The best-stocked classroom and school libraries mean little if the books are never removed from the shelves. Students must be given time to read. And, as we noted earlier, they must be given opportunities to talk about books. Not only are understandings socially constructed, but talk about books motivates students to read (Guthrie & Wigfield, 2000). Be a reader yourself, and share what you are reading. Teachers who are highly engaged readers create students who are highly engaged readers as they model their enthusiasm and strategic thinking about texts (Dreher, 2003).

4. *Plan for whole-group, small-group, and individual experiences with literature.* Whole-class experiences with literature contribute to the building of a community and offer opportunities for scaffolded instruction and guidance. Small-group experiences provide students with greater opportunities for interaction and negotiation of meaning. Individual reading of self-selected books respects student interests and choice and helps students develop independent reading strategies that underlie lifelong reading.

5. *At those times when you choose to provide group experiences with a particular work of literature, be sure to read the book.* Simple as it may seem, it is very important that prior to engaging students in a literature experience, you read the entire book yourself. It is not possible to plan meaningful experiences or respond to students' explorations without being familiar with the book.

6. *Identify themes, topics, or compelling issues in the book.* The themes, topics, or issues you identify will guide the experiences you plan for your students. Be prepared for the possibility, however, that during the course of discussion other ideas may emerge from the students that will take precedence over the ones you selected.

7. *Plan activities for three stages of exploration: before, during, and after reading.* Prereading activities should set the stage for personal responses to literature, activate and build relevant background knowledge and language, help students set purposes for reading, and spark students' curiosity. During-reading activities should support students' active engagement with the text, fostering comprehension and prompting personal connections and responses to ideas in the text. Postreading activities should encourage students to respond to the literature in personally meaningful ways and to think deeply about and beyond the literature.

8. *Establish an atmosphere of trust.* Students will honestly communicate their feelings, experiences, and ideas only if there is an atmosphere of trust in the classroom. You can promote trust by listening actively to the contributions of your students, respecting all student attempts to share, and allowing for a variety of interpretations of the meaning of a selection as long as the readers can support their ideas on the basis of the language in the text or their own experiences. Disagreements among students should be used to lead them back to the book to conduct a closer analysis of the author's words or to prompt them to identify and elaborate on their experiences and knowledge that may differ from those of their peers.

RATIONALE FOR SELECTION OF ACTIVITIES FOR THIS BOOK

The following questions guided our search for activities to include in this book.

1. *Will the activity promote grand conversations about books?* "Grand conversations" can be best described by contrasting them to the "gentle inquisitions" that take place in many classrooms (Bird, 1988; Edelsky, 1988; Eeds & Wells, 1989). During grand conversations, students are encouraged to think, feel, and respond to ideas, issues, events, and characters in a book. They are invited to express their opinions, and their opinions are valued. Personal involvement with the ideas contained in the book is encouraged, and individual interpretations are permissible as long as they are supported with data from the text. Grand conversations are similar to the discussions that occur in adult book groups in that the focus is on topics that are meaningful to the participants, and everyone is encouraged to contribute.

During "gentle inquisitions," on the other hand, the tone of the classroom interaction is one of "checking up" on the students. The teacher asks questions, and the students answer them. Although it is appropriate to assess students' comprehension, studies have revealed that a great deal of reading instructional time is spent asking students questions for the purpose of assessing their comprehension (Durkin, 1979; Wendler, Samuels, & Moore, 1989), and that higher-level reasoning activities, such as discussing and analyzing what has been read, are not routinely emphasized for students (Langer, Applebee, Mullis, & Foertsch, 1990). Allington (1994, p. 23) agrees that children "need substantially less interrogation and substantially more opportunities to observe and engage in conversations about books, stories, and other texts they have read."

The activities provided in this book can be used to stimulate grand conversations. They provide teachers with structures for encouraging students to express their ideas honestly and share their thoughts and experiences with their peers. Thus, they provide an alternative to the traditional question-and-answer discussion format that usually focuses on correctness, can discourage meaningful conversations, and often limits participation to the most verbal children in the class.

2. *Will the activity activate and/or develop background knowledge?* We have noted that what the reader brings to a work of literature influences his or her interaction with the literature. In fact, research reveals that a reader's experiences and knowledge provide the basis for comprehension of ideas in a text. Comprehension is said to occur only when a reader can mentally activate a schema—that is, some relevant organized knowledge of the world—that offers an adequate account of the objects, events, and relationships described in the text (Anderson, 1984).

The following sentence offered by Bransford and McCarrell (1974) illustrates this phenomenon: *The notes were sour because the seam split.* The vocabulary is not difficult and the sentence is short, yet it probably makes little sense to you. However, if you have any knowledge of bagpipes and you read this sentence in the context of bagpipes, it is no longer incomprehensible. Your schema of bagpipes accounts for all the elements in the sentence: the split seam, the sour notes, and the cause-effect relationship between the two. Failure to activate, or call to mind, an appropriate schema results in poor comprehension. An effective teacher promotes comprehension in his or her students by providing experiences that encourage them to access relevant knowledge prior to encountering a text. If students do not have the relevant background knowledge, the teacher helps the students acquire the appropriate knowledge through real-world experiences, other text or media experiences, or interactions with peers.

Many of the activities described in this book, especially those recommended for use before reading, are ideal for activating and building background knowledge. They prompt students to think and talk about experiences they have had or to articulate their opinions on topics about which they will subsequently read. Students with limited background knowledge on a particular topic will benefit from listening to the comments of peers.

3. *Will the activity prompt students to use comprehension strategies?* Good readers engage in numerous strategies as they read (Duke & Pearson, 2002; Pressley, 2002). They identify goals, overview texts prior to reading, and construct hypotheses about the content of a text. They check, and often change, their hypotheses as they read, make inferences, monitor their reading, and evaluate the text. They integrate their prior knowledge with material from the text, selectively read and reread, reflect on and summarize text, and consider the usefulness of the text. Good readers are active.

A great deal of research has demonstrated that children can be taught to engage in the strategies that good readers use and that instruction in these strategies results in enhanced comprehension. Specifically, research supports teaching students to make predictions and activate prior knowledge (Duke & Pearson, 2002), monitor their comprehension, use text structure to organize understanding and recall of text information, construct visual representations, summarize text information, answer questions about text, and ask questions about text (National Reading Panel, 2000; RAND, 2002). Additionally, evidence suggests that teaching students to integrate these comprehension strategies is highly effective.

To teach students strategies singly or in combination, literacy experts recommend a model of instruction that involves a gradual release of responsibility from the teacher to the student (Roehler & Duffy, 1984). The teacher begins by providing an explicit description of the strategies, including when and how to use them. Then, the teacher models the strategies, thinking aloud for the students as he or she reads. Next, the teacher and students engage in the strategies together, and the teacher provides feedback as the students make attempts to use the strategies. The teacher gradually releases responsibility to the students, providing less instruction and feedback as the students become more independent. Finally, students use the strategies independently, with cuing and prompting from the teacher until they autonomously apply the strategies they are learning.

The activities in this book prompt students to utilize comprehension strategies. As students participate in the activities, they actively engage with text. They make predictions and read to confirm or reject their predictions; they monitor their comprehension, noting whether they are understanding the text and identifying where clarification may be needed; they use text structures such as story elements to organize their understandings of a text; they construct visual representations to depict relationships among ideas, events, and concepts; they summarize information in a variety of ways; and they answer self-posed questions and those asked by others. Further, the activities provide numerous opportunities for students to integrate the strategies as they work with their peers in building understandings of and responding to text.

4. *Does the activity promote higher-level thinking?* Many teachers are familiar with Bloom's (1956) taxonomy of educational objectives, a hierarchical classification system identifying levels of cognitive processing or thinking. The levels of the taxonomy from lowest to highest are knowledge, comprehension, application, analysis, synthesis, and evaluation. The lower levels, knowledge and comprehension, involve the ability to recall information and to understand it. The higher levels—application, analysis, synthesis, and evaluation—involve the ability to apply information learned, classify, compare and contrast, explain ideas or concepts, create, and evaluate or judge. According to Bloom (1984), educational practices, including the selection of instructional materials and the teaching methods used, seldom rise above the knowledge level. Similar conclusions were reported in the 1990 National Assessment of Educational Progress report (Langer et al., 1990), which revealed that students appear to have great difficulty with tasks requiring them to explain or elaborate on what they read, and that activities that promote higher-level reasoning, such as discussing, analyzing, or writing about what has been read, are not emphasized routinely in U.S. classrooms. More recently, Taylor, Pearson, Clark, and Walpole (1999) reported that very small numbers of teachers in their national study asked higher-level questions about reading selections, and that when discussions occurred, which was rare, they primarily focused on facts.

The activities included in this book serve to facilitate higher-level thinking. They provide opportunities for active interchange among students and encourage students to think, talk, and write about ideas that have been or will be confronted in the reading selection. They require students to compare and contrast characters and books, diagram relationships, and support their opinions with examples from the text. Many of the activities promote creative expression.

5. *Will the activity provide opportunities for reading, writing, listening, and speaking?* It has been argued that reading must be seen as part of a child's general language development and not as a discrete skill isolated from writing, listening, and speaking. Reading, writing, listening, and speaking are interrelated and mutually supportive, and classroom experiences must reflect this. Literacy experts encourage teachers to help their students understand the connection among these language skills (DeFord, 1981; Heller, 1991; Holdaway, 1979; Raphael & McMahon, 1994; Shanahan, 1988), and researchers who observed exemplary teachers of young children noted that "the most striking feature of these teachers' instruction was the degree to which they integrated their language arts literacy program" (Tracey & Morrow, 2002, p. 228).

Each of the activities described in this book provides opportunities for the integration of the language arts. None of the activities is intended to be reproduced on paper and independently completed by silent students. Rather, the activities should serve as springboards for discussions and are designed to inspire students to articulate their ideas and listen and respond to the ideas of others. Writing may precede, accompany, or be a natural outgrowth of the speaking, listening, and reading experiences.

6. *Can the activity be used with heterogeneous groups of students?* Few would argue with the notion that all students should have the opportunity to interact with good literature. Unfortunately, however, in their efforts to meet the needs of low-achieving readers, some teachers limit these students to short prose and to worksheets and activities addressing only low-level cognitive skills. Poor readers are often isolated from their more able peers and have neither the opportunity to share in a literature experience nor the opportunity to participate in the grand conversations about books that other students enjoy. Indeed, children in low-ability groups have been shown to receive less instruction and qualitatively different instruction than children in high-ability groups (Allington, 1980, 1984, 1994; Anderson et al., 1985; Au, 2002; Bracey, 1987; Walmsley & Walp, 1989; Wuthrick, 1990). Yet, research suggests that instruction involving the use of high-quality literature can make a significant difference in low-achieving students' literacy development and that these students need opportunities for higher-level thinking and discussions about books (Li, 2004). For these and other reasons, many experts recommend that flexible grouping be implemented in classrooms.

In flexible grouping, students have opportunities to participate in a variety of grouping structures—both homogeneous and heterogeneous. New groups are created frequently and disbanded once the purposes of the group are achieved.

Interacting with peers in heterogeneous settings provides important support for students' comprehension (Raphael, 2000), partly because it reduces the limiting effect of insufficient relevant background knowledge as students can draw on the backgrounds of peers to make sense of what they read (van den Broek & Kremer, 2000). In addition, participation in grand conversations with peers of different reading abilities is important because these discussions provide a window on how others think.

One of the advantages of the activities presented in this book is that they can be easily and successfully implemented with students in heterogeneous settings. Students of all ability levels can participate in the activities. Each student can contribute and each can benefit from listening to the experiences and opinions of peers.

7. *Will English learners benefit from the activities?* Nearly 20 percent of school-age students in the United States speak a first language other than English, and in some regions the percentage exceeds 50 percent. Unfortunately, like low-achieving readers, many English learners receive instruction that focuses predominantly on word identification and low-level skills. Some become adequate decoders but because opportunities to actively, thoughtfully engage with rich text have been limited, comprehension is a significant problem (Au, 2002).

Although the educational community still has much to learn about supporting the literacy development of English learners, there are several key understandings that can guide teachers as they support students' interactions with literature as well as their English language development. These include the importance of comprehensible input, the crucial role of social interactions in low-anxiety settings, the distinction between conversational and academic language, and the value of culturally familiar literature.

English learners will have the greatest opportunity to participate fully in classroom learning experiences, while simultaneously building proficiency in the new language, if teachers make the content and language of instruction more accessible—in other words, if they provide "comprehensible input" (Krashen, 1982). Comprehensible input can be provided through the use of realia (real, concrete objects), models, visuals such as photographs and drawings, hands-on activities, and graphic organizers. In addition, comprehensibility can be increased when content is familiar. You read previously about the role of background knowledge in reading. This notion is significant as you work with English learners (Droop & Verhoeven, 1998). Students are more likely to understand text if they already know something about the content or if it reflects their experiences and lives. The more familiar the content of a work of literature, the fewer are the demands on students' linguistic abilities. Thus, activities that draw on or build students' background knowledge prior to reading support the comprehensibility of the text.

In addition to providing English learners with comprehensible input, teachers should ensure that English learners have many opportunities to interact with others. Social interaction, fundamental for all learners, is crucial for English learners. Goldenberg (1996) noted that small group settings stimulate active engagement from English learners, particularly when students are involved in what he calls "instructional conversations"—conversations that focus on joint meaning making, involve questions that have multiple responses, and encourage elaboration. Students have more frequent opportunities to talk, clarify language and ideas, and negotiate meaning in small groups. Language use is purposeful and authentic. Active interplay among participants who listen, respond verbally and nonverbally, and elaborate on one another's comments supports language and cognition. However, this active interplay will not happen unless teachers have created a nonthreatening, low-anxiety atmosphere, one in which students are willing to take risks as they experiment with language in order to communicate. Additionally, activities that spark students' interest and that value varied responses are more likely to invite participation.

Teachers who work with English learners need to be aware of the fundamental distinction between conversational and academic language (Cummins, 1994). Conversational language is used in informal social interactions. It is generally contextualized language, occurring in familiar face-to-face settings and supported by gestures, facial expressions, intonation, and the immediate communicative context itself. English learners typically develop conversational language, or basic interpersonal communicative skills, fairly quickly. On the other hand, cognitive academic language proficiency—communication that depends heavily on language, demands greater cognitive involvement, and is much less supported by interpersonal or contextual cues (i.e., it is decontextualized language)—takes much longer to acquire (Cummins, 1979). Teachers who understand the distinction between conversational and academic language will appreciate students' conversational abilities while recognizing that they may not have the academic language that will allow them to engage in thoughtful interactions with content without support. Teachers who understand the difference between conversational and academic language scaffold instruction in such a way as to facilitate students' understanding and, at the same time, attend to the development of their academic language.

As important as comprehensible input, social interactions, and teachers' support of academic language are, many argue that unless students find "themselves" in books, they may experience "aesthetic shutdown" (Athanases, 1998, p. 275). Reading about people who share the same cultural and ethnic background facilitates personal connections with books and contributes to positive attitudes toward reading (Hefflin & Barksdale-Ladd, 2001). Meier (2003, p. 247) noted that "not every book used in a multilingual, multicultural classroom needs to represent people of color or to incorporate linguistic diversity, but if bilingual children and children of color make up the majority of the class, then the majority of books used in the class should reflect that fact." Teachers should use materials that present diverse cultural groups in an authentic manner (Au, 1998).

The activities in this book support English learners' interactions with literature in that they contribute to comprehensible input by including nonlinguistic elements and drawing on and valuing students' background knowledge, provide opportunities for social interactions that motivate meaningful communication as students share their ideas and understandings and acknowledge the difference between conversational and academic language by providing scaffolds for thinking and talking about books and extending academic language. Many of the examples throughout this book are drawn from multicultural literature, and Appendix B shares award-winning multicultural literature.

English learners should not be excluded from opportunities to engage with literature. Literature provides exposure to rich language and powerful ideas that are worth thinking and talking about. And, shared literature experiences can contribute to building a classroom community where all members feel comfortable participating in the conversation.

CONCLUSION

Literature should be at the heart of our literacy programs. Not only does it support many aspects of literacy development—language, comprehension, writing, attitudes, and perceptions—it provides an excellent context for deep thinking and personal response. Literature inspires us and informs us; it nurtures our imaginations; it moves us to laughter, to tears, and to action. In the remaining chapters of this book, we provide activities that support students' rich interactions with text.

REFERENCES

Allington, R. (1980). Teacher interruption behaviors during primary-grade oral reading. *Journal of Educational Psychology, 72,* 371–377.

Allington, R. (1984). Content coverage and contextual reading in reading groups. *Journal of Reading Behavior, 16,* 85–96.

Allington, R. (1994). The schools we have. The schools we need. *The Reading Teacher, 48,* 14–29.

Almasi, J. (1995). The nature of fourth graders' sociocognitive conflicts in peer-led and teacher-led discussions of literature. *Reading Research Quarterly, 30,* 314–351.

Almasi, J. (1996). A new view of discussion. In L. Gambrell & J. Almasi (Eds.), *Lively discussions! Fostering engaged reading* (pp. 2–24). Newark, DE: International Reading Association.

Almasi, J. F., O'Flahavan, J. F., & Arya, P. (2001). A comparative analysis of student and teacher development in more and less proficient discussions of literature. *Reading Research Quarterly, 36,* 96–120.

Anderson, R. (1984). Role of the reader's schema in comprehension, learning, and memory. In R. Anderson, J. Osborn, & R. Tierney (Eds.), *Learning to read in American schools: Basal readers and content texts.* Hillsdale, NJ: Erlbaum.

Anderson, R., Hiebert, E., Scott, J., & Wilkinson, I. (1985). *Becoming a nation of readers: The report of the Commission on Reading.* Washington, DC: The National Institute of Education, U.S. Department of Education.

Athanases, S. Z. (1998). Diverse learners, diverse texts: Exploring identity and difference through literary encounters. *Journal of Literacy Research, 30,* 273–296.

Au, K. H. (1998). Social constructivism and the school literacy learning of students of diverse backgrounds. *Journal of Literacy Research, 30,* 297–319.

Au, K. H. (2002). Multicultural factors and the effective instruction of students of diverse backgrounds. In A. E. Farstrup & S. J. Samuels (Eds.), *What research has to say about reading instruction* (3rd ed., pp. 392–413). Newark, DE: International Reading Association.

Beach, R. (1993). *Reader-response theories.* Urbana, IL: National Council of Teachers of English.

Bean, T. W. (2000). Reading in the content areas: Social constructivist dimensions. In M. L. Kamil, P. B. Mosenthal, P. D. Pearson, & R. Barr (Eds.), *Handbook of reading research, volume II* (pp. 629–644). Mahwah, NJ: Erlbaum.

Bird, L. (1988). Reading comprehension redefined through literature study: Creating worlds from the printed page. *The California Reader, 21,* 9–14.

Bloom, B. (1956). *Taxonomy of educational objectives: Handbook I, cognitive domain.* New York: D. McKay.

Bloom, B. (1984). The search for methods of group instruction as effective as one-to-one tutoring. *Educational Leadership, 41* (8), 4–17.

Bracey, G. (1987). The social impact of ability grouping. *Phi Delta Kappan, 68,* 701–702.

Bransford, J. D., & McCarrell, N. S. (1974). A sketch of a cognitive approach to comprehension. In W. B. Weimer & D. S. Palermo (Eds.), *Cognition and the symbolic processes.* Hillsdale, NJ: Erlbaum.

Chomsky, C. (1972). Stages in language development and reading exposure. *Harvard Educational Review, 42,* 1–33.

Cohen, D. (1968). The effect of literature on vocabulary and reading achievement. *Elementary English, 45,* 209–213, 217.

Cummins, J. (1979). Linguistic interdependence and educational development in bilingual children. *Review of Educational Research, 49,* 222–251.

Cummins, J. (1994). Primary language instruction and the education of language minority students. In *Schooling and language minority students: A theoretical framework* (2nd ed., pp. 3–46). Sacramento: California State Department of Education.

DeFord, D. (1981). Literacy: Reading, writing, and other essentials. *Language Arts, 58,* 652–658.

DeFord, D. (1984). Classroom contexts for literacy learning. In T. Raphael (Ed.), *The context of school-based literacy* (pp. 163–180). New York: Random House.

Dreher, M. J. (2003). Motivating teachers to read. *The Reading Teacher, 56,* 338–340.

Droop, M., & Verhoeven, L. (1998). Background knowledge, linguistic complexity, and second-language reading comprehension. *Journal of Literacy Research, 30,* 253–271.

Duke, N. (1999). *The scarcity of informational text in first grade.* University of Michigan-Ann Arbor: Center for the Improvement of Early Reading Achievement.

Duke, N. K., & Pearson, P. D. (2002). Effective practices for developing reading comprehension. In A. E. Farstrup & S. J. Samuels (Eds.), *What research has to say about reading instruction* (3rd ed., pp. 205–242). Newark, DE: International Reading Association.

Durkin, D. (1979). What classroom observations reveal about reading comprehension instruction. *Reading Research Quarterly, 14,* 481–533.

Eckhoff, B. (1983). How reading affects children's writing. *Language Arts, 60,* 607–616.

Edelsky, C. (1988). Living in the author's world: Analyzing the author's craft. *The California Reader, 21,* 9–14.

Eeds, M., & Wells, D. (1989). Grand conversations: An explanation of meaning construction in literature study groups. *Research in the Teaching of English, 23,* 4–29.

Eldredge, J., & Butterfield, D. (1986). Alternatives to traditional reading instruction. *The Reading Teacher, 40,* 32–37.

Feitelson, D., Kita, B., & Goldstein, Z. (1986). Effects of listening to series stories on first graders' comprehension and use of language. *Research in the Teaching of English, 20,* 339–355.

Galda, L., & Cullinan, B. E. (2003). Literature for literacy: What research says about the benefits of using trade books in the classroom. In J. Flood, D. Lapp, J. R. Squire, & J. M. Jensen (Eds.), *Handbook of research on teaching the English language arts* (2nd ed., pp. 640–648). Mahwah, NJ: Erlbaum.

Gambrell, L. B. (2004). Shifts in the conversation: Teacher-led, peer-led, and computer-mediated discussions. *The Reading Teacher, 58,* 212–215.

Goldenberg, C. (1996). The education of language-minority students: Where are we, and where do we go from here? *The Elementary School Journal, 96,* 353–361.

Graves, M. F., Juel, C., & Graves, B. B. (2004). *Teaching reading in the 21st century* (3rd ed.). Boston: Allyn and Bacon.

Guthrie, J. T., & Wigfield, A. (2000). Engagement and motivation in reading. In M. L. Kamil, P. B. Mosenthal, P. D. Pearson, & R. Barr (Eds.), *Handbook of reading research, volume II* (pp. 403–422). Mahwah, NJ: Erlbaum.

Hagerty, P., Hiebert, E., & Owens, M. (1989). Students' comprehension, writing, and perceptions in two approaches to literacy instruction. In S. McCormick & J. Zutell (Eds.), *Cognitive and social perspectives for literacy research and instruction* (pp. 453–459). Chicago: National Reading Conference.

Hefflin, B. R., & Barksdale-Ladd, M. A. (2001). African American children's literature that helps students find themselves: Selection guidelines for grades K–3. *The Reading Teacher, 54,* 810–819.

Heller, M. (1991). *Reading-writing connections: From theory to practice.* New York: Longman.

Holdaway, D. (1979). *The foundations of literacy.* Exeter, NH: Heinemann.

Jewell, T., & Pratt, D. (1999). Literature discussions in the primary grades: Children's thoughtful discourse about books and what teachers can do to make it happen. *The Reading Teacher, 52* (8), 842–850.

Krashen, S. (1982). *Principles and practices in second language acquisition.* Oxford: Pergamon.

Lancia, P. J. (1997). Literary borrowing: The effects of literature on children's writing. *The Reading Teacher, 50,* 470–475.

Langer, J. (1995). *Envisioning literature: Literary understanding and literature instruction.* New York: Teacher College Press.

Langer, J., Applebee, A., Mullis, I., & Foertsch, M. (1990). *Learning to read in our nation's schools: Instruction and achievement in 1988 at grades 4, 8, and 12. National Assessment of Educational Progress.* Princeton, NJ: Educational Testing Service.

Larrick, N. (1987). Illiteracy starts too soon. *Phi Delta Kappan, 69,* 184–189.

Li, G. (2004). Perspectives on struggling English language learners: Case studies of two Chinese-Canadian children. *Journal of Literacy Research, 36,* 31–72.

Meier, T. (2003). "Why can't she remember that?" The importance of storybook reading in multilingual, multicultural classrooms. *The Reading Teacher, 57,* 242–252.

Morrow, L. M. (1992). The impact of a literature-based program on literacy achievement, use of literature, and attitudes of children from minority backgrounds. *Reading Research Quarterly, 27,* 250–275.

Morrow, L. M., & Gambrell, L. B. (2000). Literature-based reading instruction. In M. L. Kamil, P. B. Mosenthal, P. D. Pearson, & R. Barr (Eds.), *Handbook of reading research, volume II* (pp. 563–586). Mahwah, NJ: Erlbaum.

Morrow, L. M., O'Connor, E., & Smith, J. (1990). Effects of a story reading program on the literacy development of at risk kindergarten children. *Journal of Reading Behavior, 22,* 255–275.

Nagy, W., Herman, P., & Anderson, R. (1985). Learning words from context. *Reading Research Quarterly, 20,* 233–253.

National Reading Panel. (2000). *Teaching children to read: An evidence-based assessment of scientific research literature on reading and its implications for reading instruction* (NIH Publication No. 00-4769). Washington, DC: U.S. Government Printing Office.

Palmer, B. M., Codling, R. M., & Gambrell, L. B. (1994). In their own words: What elementary students have to say about motivation to read. *The Reading Teacher, 48,* 176–178.

Pressley, M. (2002). Comprehension strategies instruction: A turn-of-the-century status report. In C. C. Block & M. Pressley (Eds.), *Comprehension instruction: Research-based best practices* (pp. 11–27). New York: Guilford.

Purcell-Gates, V., McIntyre, E., & Freppon, P. A. (1995). Learning written storybook language in school: A comparison of low-SES children in skills-based and whole-language classroom. *American Educational Research Journal, 32,* 659–685.

RAND Reading Study Group. (2002). *Reading for understanding: Toward an R & D program in reading comprehension.* Santa Monica, CA: RAND.

Raphael, T. (2000). Balancing literature and instruction: Lessons from the Book Club Project. In B. Taylor, M. Graves, & P. van den Broek (Eds.), *Reading for meaning: Fostering comprehension in the middle grades* (pp. 70–94). New York: Teachers College Press.

Raphael, T., & McMahon, S. (1994). Book Club: An alternative framework for reading instruction. *The Reading Teacher, 48,* 102–116.

Richards, I. A. (1929). *Practical criticism: A study of literary judgment.* New York: Harcourt.

Roehler, L., & Duffy, G. G. (1984). Direct explanation of comprehension processes. In G. G. Duffy, L. R. Roehler, & J. Mason (Eds.), *Comprehension instruction: Perspectives and suggestions* (pp. 265–280). New York: Longman.

Rosenblatt, L. M. (1938). *Literature as exploration.* New York: Appleton-Century.

Shanahan, T. (1988). The reading-writing relationship: Seven instructional principles. *The Reading Teacher, 41,* 756–761.

Taylor, B. M., Pearson, P. D., Clark, K. F., & Walpole, S. (1999). *Beating the odds in teaching all children to read.* University of Michigan-Ann Arbor: Center for the Improvement of Early Reading Achievement.

Tracey, D. H., & Morrow, L. M. (2002). Preparing young learners for successful reading comprehension. In C. C. Block & M. Pressley (Eds.), *Comprehension instruction: Research-based best practices* (pp. 219–233). New York: Guilford.

Tunnell, M., & Jacobs, J. (1989). Using "real" books: Research findings on literature based reading instruction. *The Reading Teacher, 42,* 470–477.

van den Broek, P., & Kremer, K. (2000). The mind in action: What it means to comprehend during reading. In B. Taylor, M. Graves, & P. van den Broek (Eds.), *Reading for meaning: Fostering comprehension in the middle grades* (pp. 1–31). New York: Teachers College Press.

Vygotsky, L. (1978). *Mind in society.* Cambridge, MA: Harvard University Press.

Walmsley, S., & Walp, T. (1989). *Teaching literature in elementary school.* Albany: Center for the Learning and Teaching of Literature, University at Albany, State University of New York.

Wendler, D., Samuels, S. J., & Moore, V. (1989). The comprehension instruction of award-winning teachers, teachers with master's degrees, and other teachers. *Reading Research Quarterly, 24,* 382–401.

Wiencek, J., & O'Flahavan, J. (1994). From teacher-led to peer discussions about literature: Suggestions for making the shift. *Language Arts, 71,* 448–498.

Worthy, J. (2000). Teachers' and students' suggestions for motivating middle-school students to read. In T. Shanahan & F. V. Rodriguez-Brown (Eds.), *National Reading Conference yearbook, 49* (pp. 441–451). Chicago: National Reading Conference.

Worthy, J. (2002). What makes intermediate-grade students want to read? *The Reading Teacher, 55,* 568–569.

Wuthrick, M. (1990). Blue jays win! Crows go down in defeat! *Phi Delta Kappan, 71,* 553–556.

Yopp, H. K., & Yopp, R. H. (1999). *Primary grade students' exposure to informational text.* Paper presented at the California Reading Association's annual conference research institute, Long Beach, CA. November.

CHAPTER TWO

Prereading Activities

Prereading

Purposes

- To promote personal responses
- To activate and build background knowledge
- To develop language
- To set purposes for reading
- To arouse curiosity and motivate students to read

Activities

- Anticipation guides
- Opinionnaires/questionnaires
- Book boxes
- Book bits
- Contrast charts
- Semantic maps
- K-W-L charts
- Preview-predict-confirm
- Concrete experiences
- Picture packets
- Quickwrites from experience and speedwriting
- Quickdraws

The importance of engaging students in prereading activities cannot be overemphasized. Prereading activities can stimulate personal responses to text, activate or build relevant background knowledge and language, prompt students to set purposes for reading, and ignite an interest in the reading selection. In addition, they provide the teacher with helpful information about students' preparation to interact meaningfully with the reading selection. Although important for all children, prereading activities can be especially valuable for English learners and struggling or reluctant readers.

Prereading activities can promote personal responses to literature by signaling students that their knowledge, experiences, ideas, feelings, and beliefs matter and by prompting them to think about ideas in a book before reading about them. When students learn that what they bring to the text is valued, they are likely to continue to bring themselves to the text. When students think and talk about issues, events, or ideas in a reading selection before they read about them in the book, they may feel a greater sense of connection to the book and gain a deeper appreciation for the events, experiences, characters, and other book content.

In addition, activities conducted prior to reading a selection can serve to activate and build students' background knowledge on topics or concepts addressed in the book. As noted in Chapter One, activation of relevant knowledge is fundamental to comprehension. What readers already know about the topic of a text influences their understanding of the text. All students can benefit from activities that draw attention to and/or build relevant knowledge of a topic. As students engage in these activities with one another, knowledge is shared: Students draw on their own knowledge and learn from the knowledge of others. As readers, they will bring more to the text and, in turn, get more from it. Classrooms with children from diverse backgrounds are well positioned for rich interactions; multiple perspectives and different information and experiences related to a topic can be shared, enriching all students' knowledge.

Students who bring relevant language to the text, too, are more likely to interact meaningfully with the reading selection. Activities that highlight or build vocabulary and prompt rich discussions of text-related ideas can significantly impact comprehension and are highly appropriate for use prior to reading. As students articulate their own ideas, feelings, understandings and listen to those of others, as they seek clarification while talking with one another, as they think about words in relation to a topic, as they collaborate to make word choices, and as they respond verbally to hands-on experiences, they are building their language in a setting that is purposeful and has communication as its focus.

Prereading activities are instrumental in helping students set purposes for reading. Students may read a selection to learn more about a subject they have been discussing, answer a personal question on a topic, discover how a character will handle a conflict, learn if their experiences and feelings about an issue align with those of a character, discover the relevance of a particular object in a selection, or determine if their predictions are correct. Having set purposes for reading, students more actively engage with the selection and comprehension will be enhanced.

Prereading activities also serve to spark students' interest in the reading selection. Discussions, sharing of experiences, hands-on activities, or reactions to conflicts can arouse their curiosity about a selection. They are eager to read the text to learn what happens, to see whether their hypotheses and predictions about the text are correct, or to discover what the author has to say about a topic and whether their personal questions are addressed. We see a heightened motivation to read a book when students have thought about issues in the selection. Motivation can be the difference between engagement and disengagement, between action and inaction. Reluctant readers, in particular, need teachers who know how to stimulate their interest in a reading selection.

In this chapter, we describe twelve activities that may be used prior to reading a book, a chapter, or a passage. The first activity, the *anticipation guide,* prompts students to think about and take a stand on issues or ideas that they will later encounter. *Opinionnaires/questionnaires* are useful for tapping students' knowledge and previous related experiences as well as their beliefs and opinions on a subject. *Book boxes* and *book bits* provide students with clues about a selection. They serve to arouse curiosity and invite speculation about the characters, events, themes, or content of the book. *Contrast charts* are useful for helping students generate ideas in contrasting categories. *K-W-L charts* provide a simple format for students to identify what they know about a topic and what questions they have about the topic before reading. *Semantic maps,* graphic depictions of categorical information, serve to build and activate background knowledge. The *preview-predict-confirm* activity gives students the opportunity to preview texts in order to make predictions about their language and content. *Concrete experiences* and *picture packets* provide students with experiences or opportunities to explore objects or visuals related to content in a reading selection. *Quickwrites from experience, speedwriting,* and *quickdraws* prompt students to make connections between their knowledge or experiences and text ideas. Each of these activities can serve to pique students' curiosity about a selection, prompting them to approach it with questioning minds.

Prereading activities are a critical part of the instructional cycle and are used with the following purposes in mind:

- To invite students to respond personally to text
- To activate and build students' background knowledge on topics or concepts relevant to the selection
- To develop language
- To set purposes for reading
- To arouse students' curiosity and motivate them to read

English learners can benefit greatly from the prereading activities shared in this chapter. The frontloading of language and knowledge that occurs through prereading activities is supportive of students' successful interactions with text. Each activity provides a means for all students to communicate their individual experiences or feelings. Students engage in purposeful use of language in a setting of acceptance. English learners listen to the language of peers, and their own language production is supported by group members as they all work to clarify ideas. Relevant vocabulary is developed in authentic circumstances. Further, background knowledge, important for all learners, is especially important for English learners because it may compensate for limited English language proficiency. Background knowledge contributes to the comprehensibility of the text input. In addition, prereading activities that ignite students' interest provide the motivation for students to be persistent in their efforts to read. Students may expend considerable energy on texts they have a desire to read, even when those texts are linguistically challenging.

Prereading activities are also particularly beneficial for struggling readers because they build pertinent language and background, promote authentic uses of comprehension strategies, and provide the motivation for students to engage with text. The motivational aspects of prereading activities also can be key in bringing reluctant readers to books.

Finally, it is important to point out that prereading activities offer the teacher an opportunity to assess students. What do the students know about the topic at hand? Have they had experiences that will support their understanding of the issues or topics in the text? Do they have relevant vocabulary? Do they demonstrate any interest or curiosity in the ideas they will encounter in the reading selection? By listening closely to students, teachers will learn how much support must be provided in order to ensure meaningful interactions with the reading selection.

ANTICIPATION GUIDES

An *anticipation guide* (based on Readance, Bean, & Baldwin, 1981) is a list of statements with which the students are asked to agree or disagree. The statements are related to themes, issues, or concepts in the reading selection, and an effort is made to develop statements that will result in differences of opinion and thus lead to discussion. This activity primes students for making personal connections with the text and sparks their interest as they consider their own opinions and those of their classmates.

Several statements are presented to the students by projecting them onto a screen, writing them on a whiteboard or chart paper, or distributing them as a handout. Students are provided time to consider and respond privately to each of the statements, recording their agreement or disagreement. Then, the teacher engages the students in a discussion about the statements. Students share their agreement or disagreement by raising hands, signaling with a thumbs up or down, holding up an AGREE or DISAGREE card, or moving to a designated side of the room. The students share reasons for their responses and are encouraged to comment on their peers' responses. If an atmosphere of trust has been established in the classroom, students with minority opinions will feel comfortable sharing their thoughts.

Another way to structure the activity is to provide each student with a set of statements written on individual small strips of paper. Each student sorts the statements into two groups: those with which he or she agrees and those with which he or she disagrees. Then the students meet in groups to share their sorted strips and discuss their reasons for sorting the statements as they did.

Asking students to consider statements such as, *It is fun to be different*, can generate lively discussion and prompt students to explore and identify their own attitudes and beliefs as well as contemplate those of their classmates. Students gain an appreciation for a diversity of perspectives. When the students later encounter the issues they discussed in the reading selection, they are likely to respond at a deeper level than if they had not considered the issues before reading.

Anticipation guides for several books are presented on the next few pages. A brief summary of each book is provided for the teacher and is not intended to be shared with the students. Sample student responses are offered in Example 2.5. We are not suggesting that these are "correct" responses. They are provided only so the teacher can more fully understand the activity. Student responses will, and should, vary. In addition to indicating their agreement or disagreement with statements in an anticipation guide, students may be asked to write a brief comment in response to each statement.

Example 2.1

- **Title:** *A Fine, Fine School*
- **Author:** Sharon Creech
- **Grade Level:** K–3
- **Summary:** A principal is so pleased with his school and the wonderful learning that takes place that he decides school should be held on weekends, holidays, and during the summer too. The students and teachers, not wanting to hurt his feelings, attend school every day until young Tillie finally tells the principal there are things that should be learned outside of school as well.

Anticipation Guide

Agree   Disagree

_____ _____ 1. If you enjoy something, you should do more of it.

_____ _____ 2. The most important things to learn are taught in school.

_____ _____ 3. Very good people sometimes make bad decisions.

_____ _____ 4. You should tell the truth even if it might hurt someone's feelings.

Example 2.2

- **Title:** *Teammates*
- **Author:** Peter Golenbock
- **Grade Level:** 1–4
- **Summary:** This book describes the prejudice experienced by Jackie Robinson, the first black player in Major League baseball. It highlights his courage and the support he received from Pee Wee Reese, a white teammate.

Anticipation Guide

Agree   Disagree

_____ _____ 1. Staying away from people who are cruel to you is a good idea.

_____ _____ 2. It's fun to be different.

_____ _____ 3. When you are very good at something, people like you.

		4. Sometimes one person can make a difference in the world.
_____	_____	5. If everybody is being cruel to someone, there's probably a good reason.

Example 2.3 _____

- **Title:** *Flying Solo*
- **Author:** Ralph Fletcher
- **Grade Level:** 4–8
- **Summary:** The students in Mr. Fabiano's sixth-grade class decide not to report that the substitute has failed to show up. The students, including Rachel, who has been mute since a classmate's death, and Bastion, who is struggling with an impending move, learn much about themselves and one another during the day.

Anticipation Guide

Agree   Disagree

_____	_____	1. Students are capable of running a class without a teacher.
_____	_____	2. You should try to avoid thinking about things that bother you.
_____	_____	3. It is important to do what is best for you, even if it is not good for someone else.
_____	_____	4. On important decisions, the majority should rule.

Example 2.4 _____

- **Title:** *Tuck Everlasting*
- **Author:** Natalie Babbitt
- **Grade Level:** 4–8
- **Summary:** Ten-year-old Winnie Foster stumbles upon the Tuck family's secret: They will live forever. Those who drink from a spring in the woods near the Fosters' home—which the Tucks did inadvertently 87 years ago—cannot die. In this thought-provoking story, Winnie faces a number of moral dilemmas and ultimately accomplishes something important.

Anticipation Guide

Agree   Disagree

_____	_____	1. It would be wonderful to live forever.
_____	_____	2. You should never do something that your parents have forbidden.
_____	_____	3. Some secrets are so important that it is acceptable to do anything in order to keep them.

_____ . _____	4.	People should have the right to sell products even if they are harmful.
_____ _____	5.	It is OK to hurt one person to protect many.

Example 2.5

- ■ **Title:** *Dragonwings*
- ■ **Author:** Laurence Yep
- ■ **Grade Level:** 5–8
- ■ **Summary:** An eight-year-old boy travels from China to the United States to be with his father whom he has never seen. There, he confronts prejudice and discrimination as well as his own misperceptions about Americans. He watches his father struggle toward achieving his dream to fly. The story takes place in the early 1900s and was inspired by the actual account of a Chinese immigrant who built a flying machine in 1909.

Anticipation Guide

Agree   Disagree

Agree	Disagree		
_X_	_____	1.	It would be exciting to move to a new country. *I think you'd see a lot of interesting things in another country.*
_____	_X_	2.	Discrimination and prejudice often work both ways between immigrants and native peoples. *Usually the people already living in a country don't like newcomers, but newcomers want to be friends.*
_____	_X_	3.	A father has a duty to always protect his children from harm. *Parents should take care of their children, but eventually children must take care of themselves.*
_X_	_____	4.	People should not spend energy working on unrealistic goals. *If it's unrealistic, it's stupid for someone to spend time on it. He should find another goal.*

Completed anticipation guides may be saved for reconsideration after a selection has been read. The format of the anticipation guide can be easily modified to include a single column for anticipation responses in which students put a plus or a minus symbol (or a smiling or frowning face) indicating agreement or disagreement, and a second column for reaction responses. Students complete the second column after reading the selection.

Upon completing the activity the second time, students may discover that their attitudes and understandings have changed as a result of their reading.

OPINIONNAIRES/QUESTIONNAIRES

Opinionnaires/questionnaires (Reasoner, 1976) are useful tools for helping readers examine their own values, attitudes, opinions, or related experiences before they read the book. Constructing an opinionnaire/questionnaire is very much like constructing an anticipation guide. The teacher first identifies themes, ideas, or major events around which to focus discussion. Then the teacher generates a series of questions to tap students' opinions, attitudes, or past experiences related to those themes. Some items on the opinionnaires/questionnaires may be open-ended, whereas others may be more structured and offer students a checklist of possible responses.

The purpose of this activity is to facilitate students' thinking about their own attitudes and experiences related to selected issues, not to elicit "correct" responses. The teacher should be accepting of all responses and avoid valuing some opinions more than others.

We have seen teachers respond to students in a way that suggests there is a single correct response, and we have seen students become increasingly uncomfortable in these situations. It is apparent in these cases that the teacher is not truly interested in the students' opinions, and the teacher's behavior serves as a roadblock to the grand conversations the activity could have prompted.

The opinionnaire/questionnaire depicted in Example 2.6 provides a structure for students to talk about being different. When they subsequently hear or read the story *Stargirl*, they are more likely to appreciate the story events. Note that extra spaces are included so that students may insert their own ideas.

Example 2.6 _____

- **Title:** *Stargirl*
- **Author:** Jerry Spinelli
- **Grade Level:** 4–6
- **Summary:** A new girl attracts much attention at Mica High School because she is so different—she wears unusual clothes, behaves in unusual ways, and has an unusual name. Leo Borlock falls in love with her the moment he sees her but soon tries to convince her to become "normal." *Stargirl* is a story of popularity and conformity.

Opinionnaire/Questionnaire

1. People who are different from their peers
   - _____ should be avoided because they are strange.
   - _____ should be taught to be like everyone else.
   - _____ should be appreciated for being different.
   - _____ should be laughed at because they are different.
   - _____ are just trying to get attention.
   - _____ _____
   - _____ _____

2. To shun someone means to act like he or she does not exist. What would you do if people shunned you?

_____ Tell an adult.

_____ Try to convince them to talk to you.

_____ Ignore them.

_____ Change your behavior, clothes, or hairstyle to see if they like the new you.

_____ _____

3. In the first column, rate the behavior on a scale of 1 (least) to 5 (most) in terms of kindness. In the second column, indicate with a Y (yes) or N (no) whether the behavior is something you would consider doing.

_____ _____ Giving birthday gifts

_____ _____ Helping someone carry bags of groceries

_____ _____ Cheering for the opposing team in a sporting event

_____ _____ Teaching someone to dance

_____ _____ Spying on neighbors

_____ _____ _____

4. If you could choose a name for yourself, what name would you choose? Why?

_____

_____

Students may use the opinionnaire/questionnaire to poll others (e.g., students in other classrooms, parents) to discover what they believe. The data may then be compiled for class summary and analysis.

Example 2.7 _____

- **Title:** *Roll of Thunder, Hear My Cry*
- **Author:** Mildred Taylor
- **Grade Level:** 6–8
- **Summary:** Set in the South during the Depression, this story relates the struggles of a black family and its encounters with hate and prejudice.

Opinionnaire/Questionnaire

Listed below are a few incidents that make some people feel bad. Which of them would make you feel bad?

_____ When someone you love is ashamed of you

_____ When people call you names

_____ When people act as if they are better than you

_____ When you are punished for something you did that you should not have done

_____ When someone stares at you

_____ _____

_____ _____

What would you do if you were tricked out of a favorite possession by someone you knew?

_____ Cry.

_____ Tell your parents and ask for their help.

_____ Tell that person's parents and ask for their help.

_____ Tell all your friends so they won't be nice to that person.

_____ Get it back somehow.

_____ Pretend you didn't like the possession anyway.

_____ Decide you didn't deserve the possession.

_____ Trick that person out of something to show him or her how it feels.

_____ _____

_____ _____

If you were in a store and the clerk who was waiting on you stopped helping you and turned to assist two other people, what would you do?

_____ Wait patiently.

_____ Leave and go somewhere else.

_____ Leave and tell your parents.

_____ Complain to the manager.

_____ Demand that the clerk finish helping you.

_____ _____

_____ _____

A boy in your class is always bothering you, acting smarter than you, and getting into mischief. Which of the following describe what you would do?

_____ Feel sorry for him.

_____ Try to be his friend and help him change.

_____ Ignore him.

_____ Tell him you don't like his behavior.

_____ Hope someone catches him someday.

_____ Tell on him.

_____ _____

_____ _____

If he came to you for help, what would you do?

_____ Tell him "No way!"

_____ Help him.

_____ Laugh at him.

_____ Pretend you'd help him, then don't.

_____ _____

_____ _____

As with the anticipation guides, opinionnaires/questionnaires may be redistributed after students have read the book. Students may examine whether their reponses have changed, and if so, why they have changed.

BOOK BOXES

The book box activity stimulates thinking about a selection and builds anticipation as students are shown objects that serve as clues to a text's content. Students use these clues to make predictions about the reading selection.

The teacher begins by informing students that they soon will be reading a new book and that there are several objects in a box that are somehow related to the book. The teacher draws one object from the box at a time. Students identify the object—this is particularly important when it is unusual or unfamiliar—and in small groups talk about the object and begin to generate predictions about the content of the book. What does the object suggest about the book? After several predictions are shared with the entire group, a second object is drawn from the box. Students once again engage in discussion, first in small groups and then as they share their thinking with the entire group. As each new object is drawn from the box, students' predictions about the selection are extended or revised. Once students have seen all the objects, they make final predictions that must account for each object. It is important that students are given ample time to talk with one another and to share their evolving visions of the selection. Listening to the experiences, knowledge, and thinking of peers supports all students as they consider the objects and possible relationships among them.

Examples 2.8, 2.9, and 2.10 provide suggestions for objects to be included in book boxes for *Officer Buckle and Gloria* by Peggy Rathman, *The First Strawberries* by Joseph Bruchac, and *Holes* by Louis Sachar. Objects may be drawn from the book box in any order.

Example 2.11 provides a format to record clues and predictions if the teacher would like students to record their thinking in writing. Students identify each object as it is revealed, engage in a small-group discussion, and record two predictions—individually or as a group—before their thinking is shared with classmates. Developing two predictions about the content of a text after each clue stretches students' thinking and encourages elaboration in their discussion as they consider alternatives that would account for each of the clues.

The book box activity is valuable for a number of reasons. Students bring their experiences and knowledge to discussions with peers, and students' mental activity becomes public as they generate and explain predictions and share their thinking with one another. The use of objects is motivating and provides nonverbal support for understanding. Also, higher-order thinking is demanded as students consider the relationships among a number of objects and evaluate the adequacy of their predictions as additional information is revealed.

Example 2.8 _____

- **Title:** *Officer Buckle and Gloria*
- **Author:** Peggy Rathman
- **Grade Level:** K–3
- **Summary:** The children of Napville School are bored by Officer Buckle's safety rule presentations until he is joined by a canine partner, Gloria. Officer Buckle discovers that the dog is the reason for his enormous success and dissolves the partnership, leaving Gloria to attend the school assemblies by herself. He soon learns that they need each other and happily shares Safety Tip #101: Always stick with your buddy.

Objects in the Book Box

Dog collar	Thumbtack
Police badge	Helmet

Example 2.9 _____

- **Title:** *The First Strawberries*
- **Author:** Joseph Bruchac
- **Grade Level:** K–3
- **Summary:** This Cherokee legend tells the origin of strawberries. A woman, angry at her husband for his harsh words when she is picking flowers rather than cooking their meal, walks away from him. He follows her but cannot catch up to her. The sun helps the man by causing strawberries to grow along her path. She stops to eat them and their sweetness reminds her of the happiness she shared with her husband.

Objects in the Book Box

Figurines of a husband and wife (wedding attire makes this relationship explicit)

A bunch of flowers

Some strawberries

Example 2.10

- **Title:** *Holes*
- **Author:** Louis Sachar
- **Grade Level:** 4–8
- **Summary:** When given the choice between camp and traditional prison, the family of Stanley Yelnats sends him to Camp Green Lake to serve a sentence for a crime he did not commit. There, he and the other boys dig holes in the dry hard dirt every day. Unknown to the boys, the warden hopes to uncover a treasure left by a notorious bandit a century ago. This eventful and sometimes humorous tale that weaves the past with the present is a Newbery Medal winner.

Objects in the Book Box

Shovel	Sneakers
Onion	Jar of peaches
Handcuffs, sheriff's badge, or some item to represent the law	Tube of lipstick
	Small container of dirt

Example 2.11

- **Title:** *Bananas!*
- **Author:** Jacqueline Farmer
- **Grade Level:** 2–5
- **Summary:** Readers learn in this informational and sometimes humorous text about the nutritional value of bananas, how and where they are grown and distributed, and their history.

Objects in the Book Box

Banana	Twine
Magnifying glass	Plastic bag
Fork	Apple

Clue #1: *banana*

Prediction #1: *The book is about the importance of eating fruits and vegetables.*

Prediction #2: *This is a recipe book about different kinds of breads, including banana bread.*

Clue #2: *plastic bag*

Prediction #1: *People are shopping at a grocery store and are putting bananas in a plastic bag.*

Prediction #2: *Bananas are being placed in plastic bags to help them ripen faster.*

Clue #3: *fork*

Prediction #1: *Some people went shopping and brought home bananas in a plastic bag. They set the table with knives, spoons, and forks, and eat bananas as part of their meal.*

Prediction #2: *The book is about the different ways people eat bananas. After bringing home bananas in a plastic bag from the marketplace, people in some parts of the world cut them up and eat them with a fork.*

Clue #4: *twine*

Prediction #1: *Bananas have been rotting and have fallen to the ground. The farmers use special forks to pick up the rotting bananas and put them in plastic bags. They use twine to tie the bag.*

Prediction #2: *A worker has brought his sack lunch to a dusty location. He keeps his food and utensils in a plastic bag and ties twine around the bag to keep the contents clean.*

Clue #5: *magnifying glass*

Prediction #1: *Scientists are using magnifying glasses to inspect bananas for dangerous bacteria. They cannot handle the bananas so use forks to hold them. Any banana found to be carrying bacteria is put inside a plastic bag and the bag is tied closed with the twine.*

Prediction #2: *Some people fry bananas. The magnifying glass may be used to start a fire for cooking. The bag and twine were used to transport the bananas from a banana plantation to a marketplace. Someone has bought bananas and is cooking them. They will be eaten with a fork.*

Clue #6: *apple*

Prediction #1: *The book is about nutritious foods, including apples and bananas. Before going to a market, foods are inspected with a magnifying glass to see if they are carrying bacteria or poisons. The bag and twine are used to store bananas on the way to market. The book shares one way of eating apples and bananas—as part of a fruit salad. The fork is used to eat the cut-up pieces of fruit.*

Prediction #2: *This book is about conducting experiments with food. Apples and bananas are put in a plastic bag that is tied closed with a string and left to rot. The fork is used to mash the rotting food to get a better view of it. The magnifying glass is used to observe the decay and fruit flies.*

BOOK BITS

Book bits are similar to book boxes in that bits of information from a reading selection are shared with students before they read. Instead of objects, however, sentences or phrases from the text are shared. This sharing of bits of text arouses curiosity and stimulates thinking about the text.

The teacher prepares for this activity by selecting sentences or phrases from the text and writing each on a separate small strip of paper. The teacher should select as many sentences or phrases as there are students so everyone can participate and make a unique contribution to a group sharing of information. The book bits should reveal enough about the text to support understanding, but not so much as to limit thinking and hypothesizing about the selection.

The students are given a book bit and told that the book bits are all from the same reading selection. Each student reads his or her book bit silently and reflects on it for a moment. The teacher should make certain that students are able to read their book bit and should assist struggling readers and English learners as needed to ensure their success with this activity. After reading their book bit to themselves, the students are asked to think about the impressions they are beginning to formulate about the reading selection and to write their initial thoughts. What might the selection be about? What do they think they know about any characters? What do they think is happening or will happen? Do they have any information about the setting?

At a signal, the students move around the room, find a partner, and read their book bit to their partner. No discussion occurs at this time. Students simply read aloud their book bits to one another. After reading, students move on to find a new partner with whom to share their book bits. Once students have had the opportunity to share with three or four partners (or fewer or more, depending on the size of the group), the teacher asks them to return to their seats and quickly write any new impressions of the text based on information they acquired by listening to their partners' book bits. At a signal, students again circulate around the room and share their book bit with new partners. The teacher should call time before students hear all of the book bits.

After a final opportunity to record ideas about the text, students meet in small groups or pairs to pool their information. Because each student will likely have acquired information that other group members did not, every student can participate in the conversation and make contributions to the discussion. The pooled information is recorded on a piece of paper. If the reading selection is narrative, the teacher may suggest that each group fold a piece of paper into thirds and record information and speculations in three categories: characters, setting, and plot. See Example 2.15.

Once students have completed this phase of the activity, each small group shares its information with the entire class and the teacher records the information on a large chart or overhead transparency. Students may be surprised to learn of a character, setting, or plot element that their small group had not encountered in their sharing of book bits. Or, they may have information that supports the ideas generated by another group. Or, they may have put pieces of information together in different ways to reach different conclusions about the text. After the whole-group sharing, volunteers may read aloud or comment on their individual writing, which should reflect the evolution of their thinking and hypothesis generation about the reading selection.

If sentences are carefully selected, students will form a number of plausible impressions and hypotheses about the text. If the sentences have

revealed too much, the students' responses will converge. Notice that in Example 2.12, the word *fireflies* does not appear in any of the book bits. This was a deliberate decision on the part of the teacher. Had the word appeared in a book bit (or had the teacher shared the title of the book), the students' thinking would have narrowed very quickly and their opportunities to build interpretations would have been limited. Instead, students formed a variety of hypotheses about the selection as they read their own strip and then gathered information from peers. Their initial impressions may have had to be abandoned in favor of new ones that better accounted for the information they were gathering, and their interpretations continued to be revised as they obtained more and more information from their peers.

Example 2.12

- **Title:** *Fireflies!*
- **Author:** Julie Brinckloe
- **Grade Level:** K–3
- **Summary:** A young boy and his friends capture fireflies in glass jars and are delighted to watch them glow. As the light in the jar begins to dim, the boy tearfully realizes that he should set his fireflies free or they will die.

Book Bits
(for a group of seven students)

It was growing dark.

Something flickered there.

I poked holes in the top of the jar with Momma's scissors.

We ran like crazy.

I shut my eyes tight and put the pillow over my head.

The jar glowed like moonlight.

"Catch them, catch them!" we cried.

Example 2.13

- **Title:** *Thunder Cake*
- **Author:** Patricia Polacco
- **Grade Level:** K–3
- **Summary:** Drawing from her own experiences, Polacco shares the story of a young girl whose grandmother helps her overcome her fear of thunder. Babuska and her granddaughter locate the recipe and the ingredients to make Thunder Cake, which they complete just as the storm arrives.

Book Bits

1-2-3-4-5-6-7-8-9-10

"I am here, child."

I was scared as we walked down the path.

"Eight miles, child," Grandma croaked.

"Now we have to get chocolate and sugar and flour from the dry shed."

We measured the ingredients.

This time it lit the whole sky.

"Only a very brave person could have done all them things."

Example 2.14

- **Title:** *The Great Gilly Hopkins*
- **Author:** Katherine Paterson
- **Grade Level:** 4–8
- **Summary:** Gilly Hopkins has bounced from one foster home to another and has not allowed herself to love anyone. The eleven-year-old is bright, tough, and defiant. Gilly begins to soften under the care of Maime Trotter and, although she fights it, she cannot stop herself from growing fond of Trotter's other foster child, William Ernest, and their blind neighbor, Mr. Randolph.

Book Bits
(for a class of eighteen students)

"This will be your third home in less than three years."

"Will you do me a favor, Gilly? Try to get off on the right foot?"

Gilly carefully spread the gum under the handle of the left-hand door as a sticky surprise for the next person who might try to open it.

She turned her back on them. That would show them.

Oh, why did it have to be so hard? Other kids could be with their mothers all the time.

I don't need help from anybody.

"That was Mr. Randolph. He can't see a thing. You've got to go back and bring him by the hand, so he won't fall."

They continued to read that way. He would listen blissfully for a while and then join, turning her single voice into the sound of a choir.

"She's a handsome reader, all right."

It was only a matter of getting back into Mr. Randolph's house and getting the rest of the money. There was sure to be more.

She wasn't going to let a bunch of low-class idiots think they were smarter than she was.

The look on Trotter's face was the one Gilly had, in some deep part of her, longed to see all her life, but not from someone like Trotter.

"You and I are two of the angriest people I know."

Her heart was pumping crazily. She made herself sit down.

People were so dumb sometimes you almost felt bad to take advantage of them—but not too bad.

If she didn't watch herself, she'd start liking the little jerk.

She was not going to panic. He couldn't see. Of course, he couldn't see.

She had known that it never pays to attach yourself to something that is likely to blow away.

Example 2.15

- **Title:** *Everything on a Waffle*
- **Author:** Paula Horvath
- **Grade Level:** 4–8
- **Summary:** When eleven-year-old Primrose Squarp's father and mother are lost at sea, first Miss Perfidy (who charges by the hour), then Uncle Jack, and, for a short while, a foster family take responsibility for her. Primrose is certain that her parents are still living and trying to return home. She interacts with a variety of quirky characters and finds some comfort with Miss Bowzer, the cook and owner of a restaurant who serves everything on a waffle. Each chapter of this wonderful book of hope concludes with a recipe.

Book Bits

I knew my parents were coming home someday but in the meantime I did miss my home.

"I'm not miserable all the time. Sometimes I get these bursts of joy."

I am eleven years old.

One June day a typhoon arose at sea that blew the rain practically perpendicular to our house.

The fishing boat never came back to shore.

Uncle Jack asked me if I minded moving but I could not shake the sense that none of it mattered very much.

When school started, my real troubles began.

A group of girls began to follow me and make jeering noises at me.

"Now that's true love and it's rare as rare can be."

At the end of September the rains began. There were fewer and fewer days when I could go to sit on a dock to wait for my parents without getting drenched.

The playground became less safe as my classmates lost patience with me completely.

We walked silently the rest of the way to the jail.

"I'm sorry, Primrose, but we've got a full restaurant tonight for some reason and it's a madhouse in here."

"And we're all so happy here in a small town."

"Everyone wants to sell," said Uncle Jack. "It's just a matter of price."

I heard the long blast of a truck horn and saw big wheels. Then nothing.

He was fighting those Child Protective Services folks tooth and claw for me, and calling constantly with progress reports.

The week before Christmas, Uncle Jack got out of the hospital and he and I took long therapeutic walks on the beach.

"Children who have had emotional upsets sometimes act out and need special care."

When Miss Perfidy answered the door, I noticed that she had her dress on backwards.

For the first time it occurred to me that Miss Perfidy, who must be in the neighborhood of 104 years old, might be failing.

"A fisherman on shore saw me and yelled and a bunch of men came running and untangled me and got me back onto the dock."

Then we formed the dough into rolls and Miss Bowzer lent me a pan to take them home in.

Then Miss Honeycutt started telling Uncle Jack that she never thought he should have been asked to take a child on.

"I don't know what you think the story of Jonah is about, Miss Perfidy," I said. "But to me it is about how hopeful the human heart is."

Miss Perfidy often stalked off when I was in the middle of a sentence.

In Coal Harbour there was whaling and fishing and the navy.

He pulled out a yellow macintosh and, with a face full of pity, handed it to me.

We entered the sheriff's office. Beyond his desk were two cells, clean but spare.

This is perhaps the easiest recipe of all.

Characters	*Setting*	*Plot*
■ *Miss Honeycutt* ■ *A teacher* ■ *A child of eleven* ■ *Uncle Jack* ■ *Miss Perfidy, an old woman* ■ *A sheriff*	■ *Near the ocean* ■ *A small town* ■ *A fishing village* ■ *A restaurant* ■ *A jail* ■ *A school* ■ *The fall*	■ *People are cooking.* ■ *Someone is a criminal.* ■ *There is a terrible storm.* ■ *A child is in danger.* ■ *A group of girls makes fun of someone.* ■ *Someone is having problems at school.* ■ *Someone's parents are gone.* ■ *An accident involving a truck happens.*

CONTRAST CHARTS

Contrast charts are used to facilitate students' thinking about ideas prior to encountering them in a text. Contrast charts are simple to develop, requiring only that the teacher identify theme-related contrasting categories under which students list ideas. For example, before reading about Karana, who lived alone on an island for years in *Island of the Blue Dolphins*, by Scott O'Dell, students list the advantages and disadvantages of living alone. As students consider two sides of an issue, they engage in higher-order thinking.

Contrast charts may be generated by the class as a whole, small groups of students, or individuals. We recommend that students be given a few minutes to individually consider the issues and record any thoughts that come to mind. Then, students may work in small groups to develop a group contrast chart by listing their ideas in two columns. Students benefit from interacting with one another as they listen to and explain ideas. Each group shares its chart with classmates. Contrast charts may be saved and revisited as students read the selection.

Example 2.16 _____

- **Title:** *Alexander and the Terrible, Horrible, No Good, Very Bad Day*
- **Author:** Judith Viorst
- **Grade Level:** K–3
- **Summary:** Alexander has a horrible day when one thing after another goes wrong for him.

Contrast Chart

Have you ever heard people say, "That made my day!" or "That ruined my day"? They are referring to events that happened that make them feel especially good or particularly miserable and cranky. List some things that could happen to you that could make your day either good or bad.

Good Day	Bad Day
1.	1.
2.	2.
3.	3.
4.	4.
5.	5.
6.	6.

Example 2.17

- **Title:** *Stuart Little*
- **Author:** E. B. White
- **Grade Level:** 4–6
- **Summary:** This story tells the humorous adventures of a two-inch mouse who is born into a human family.

Contrast Chart

What would it be like if you were two inches tall? List some things that would be difficult to do. List some things that would be easy to do.

Difficult	Easy
1.	1.
2.	2.
3.	3.
4.	4.
5.	5.
6.	6.

Example 2.18

- **Title:** *Things Not Seen*
- **Author:** Andrew Clements
- **Grade Level:** 4–8
- **Summary:** Fifteen-year-old Bobby wakes up one morning to discover that he is invisible. His frantic parents—a physicist and a university professor—decide it is best not to tell anyone while they try to figure out what happened and how to reverse it. Officials become suspicious when Bobby stops attending school and his parents run out of

excuses. Bobby tells a blind girl his problem and, with her help, the problem is solved.

Contrast Chart

Advantages of Being Invisible	**Disadvantages of Being Invisible**
You can eavesdrop easily.	*No one notices you.*
You don't have to wash your hair, put on makeup, or wear nice clothes.	*You can no longer participate in normal activities.*
You can make faces at people and they won't know.	*You don't matter to people.*
You can go places you normally wouldn't be permitted to go.	

K-W-L CHARTS

Another activity that helps students access their background knowledge on a topic is the K-W-L (know, want to know, learned) chart developed by Ogle (1986). The K-W-L chart is used before and after reading or listening to a selection that contains some factual content. Prior to interacting with the selection, the students brainstorm and write on a chart what they *know* about a topic. The pooling of information helps students gain familiarity with the content and vocabulary of a subject as they draw on their own knowledge and learn from their peers. As a result, students will be better prepared for interacting with the text.

In a second column, students record what they *want to know* about the topic. When students identify questions, they are developing purposes for reading and a personal connection with the text is facilitated. The discussions that occur as the first two columns of the chart are completed reveal the extent of students' familiarity with a topic. If students' knowledge and relevant vocabulary are limited, the teacher may choose to develop students' background before reading the selection by sharing other texts, engaging in class discussions, viewing videos, conducting Internet searches, or providing direct experiences with the content.

Example 2.19 shows the two columns students completed prior to their reading of the poem "Honeybees" in *Joyful Noise,* by Paul Fleischman. Students recorded what they know about honeybees in the first column and what they want to know in the second column. Once the selection is read, students record in a third column what they have *learned* about the topic and correct any inaccurate information listed in the first column.

Example 2.19 _____

- ■ **Title:** "Honeybees" from *Joyful Noise*
- ■ **Author:** Paul Fleischman
- ■ **Grade Level:** K–6
- ■ **Summary:** This poem, one of a collection of poems about insects, describes the activities of the queen and worker honeybees.

K-W-L Chart
"Honeybees"

What We Know	**What We Want to Know**
Make honey	*How is the queen different?*
Live in hives	*Who lays the eggs?*
Have a queen	*How many are laid at a time?*
Sting	*How far away do bees fly from their hives?*
	Why does the sting hurt so much?

Example 2.20

- **Title:** *Marshes & Swamps*
- **Author:** Gail Gibbons
- **Grade Level:** 1–3
- **Summary:** After explaining the difference between marshes and swamps, the author describes various types of marshes and swamps, including how they are formed, where they are found in the United States, the life they support, and their importance.

K-W-L Chart
Marshes & Swamps

What We Know	**What We Want to Know**
Alligators and crocodiles live in swamps.	*What is the difference between a marsh and a swamp?*
Marshes and swamps are wet.	*What lives in a swamp?*
There are swamps in Florida.	*What lives in a marsh?*
Some people try to protect marshes and swamps.	*Do alligators and crocodiles live in marshes?*
Some birds need marshes and swamps to survive.	*Are there snakes in marshes and swamps?*

Example 2.21

- **Title:** *An American Plague: The True and Terrifying Story of the Yellow Fever Epidemic of 1793*
- **Author:** Jim Murphy
- **Grade Level:** 6 and up
- **Summary:** In 1793, a devastating yellow fever epidemic swept through Philadelphia. In this dramatic account, readers learn about the politics, social issues, and state of medical knowledge and health care in eighteenth-century America.

K-W-L Chart
Epidemics

What We Know	**What We Want to Know**	**What We Learned**
————————	————————	————————
————————	————————	————————
————————	————————	————————
————————	————————	————————
————————	————————	————————
————————	————————	————————
————————	————————	————————
————————	————————	————————
————————	————————	————————
————————	————————	————————

It is important that the teacher restrict use of this activity to books that contain accurate information. Students should not be asked what they know and what they have learned about whales from a work of fiction that presents whales that chat with one another and have cute personalities. The wonderful story of *Gilberto and the Wind,* by Marie Hall Ets, anthropomorphizes the wind, using phrases such as *Wind likes my soap bubbles* and *Wind is all tired out* that clearly are inappropriate to include on a K-W-L chart. Therefore, the activity should not be used with this particular book.

By no means, however, should this activity be used exclusively with nonfiction. Many works of fiction have considerable factual content. In *Johnny Tremain,* by Esther Forbes, students learn a great deal about the Revolutionary War. In *Where the Red Fern Grows,* by Wilson Rawls, students learn about life in the Ozarks. In *Miracles on Maple Hill,* by Virginia Sorensen, students learn about the production of maple syrup. The teacher must be familiar with the reading selection and be confident that information presented about a topic under consideration is accurate before using it in a K-W-L chart.

It is likely that a number of questions generated by the students will not be addressed by the reading selection. Students should be encouraged to pursue other sources of information. Ogle (1986, p. 567) said that this helps students recognize the "priority of their personal desire to learn over simply taking in what the author has chosen to include." She suggested adding a fourth column (K-W-L-H) in which students list how they will obtain the information (D. Ogle, personal communication, December 2, 1994).

Another modification of this versatile chart, the KWLA, is the addition of a column on *affect* (Mandeville, 1994). This column can be completed before, during, or after reading. Before reading, students use the "A" column to share their feelings about the topic. During or after reading, students use this column to respond to the information they have learned—recording emotional reactions, indicating what they find most interesting in the selection, identifying parts in the reading they like the most or least, or noting why some information is especially important to them.

This linking of affective and cognitive domains has tremendous potential to spark students' interest in the factual information presented in many books, and Mandeville suggests that students who attach their own importance and personal relevance to information are likely to comprehend and remember the information better.

The discussions that are prompted by this activity can provide the teacher with information that may influence instructional decisions. For instance, if students have limited relevant background knowledge or vocabulary, the teacher may choose to provide instruction that builds understandings of concepts in the reading selection. If students demonstrate little enthusiasm for the topic, the teacher may plan activities to stimulate curiosity or help the students make connections between themselves and the topic that may motivate them to read.

SEMANTIC MAPS

Semantic maps, sometimes referred to as *clusters* or *semantic webs,* are graphic displays of categorized information. They may be used to build vocabulary and activate and organize students' background knowledge on a topic (Farnan, Flood, & Lapp, 1994; Johnson & Pearson, 1984; Johnson, Pittelman, & Heimlich, 1986). They give students anchor points to which new concepts they will encounter can be attached (McNeil, 1987). To make a semantic map, the teacher first writes and encircles a term that is central to the reading selection on the board or chart paper. In a selection about schools, for example, the teacher might write the word *school* in the middle of the board. He or she next generates categories related to the central concept. For our school example, he or she might write *rooms, people,* and *studies.* Each is encircled and lines are drawn from the categories to the central concept of *school* to indicate a relationship. Then the teacher elicits from the students exemplars, details, or subordinate ideas for each of the categories. Within the category of *people,* for example, the students may list *children, teachers, principal,* and so on. These terms are written in the category circles. The teacher leads the students in a discussion about the terms and their relationships. Research suggests that this discussion is key to the effectiveness of the technique (Stahl & Vancil, 1986). Once a map is generated, the class may want to save it to refer to during or after reading. At any point the map may be modified to reflect new information or ideas.

Another way to develop a semantic map is to have the students brainstorm and record the subordinate ideas after being told the central concept and then to group them into categories and label the categories. This approach is similar to Taba's (1967) list-group-label technique for concept development.

The use of semantic maps prior to reading has been found to result in better story recall in less-able readers than the use of the more traditional directed reading technique in which new content, new vocabulary, and the purpose for reading a selection are discussed prior to reading (Sinatra, Stahl-Gemake, & Berg, 1984). The use is supported by schema theory described in Chapter One. Schemata (plural of *schema*) are networks of knowledge that readers store in their minds. Semantic maps help students tap those networks, integrate new information, and restructure existing networks. Because semantic maps provide a visual display of concepts and the relationships among them and they tap, honor, and extend students' background knowledge and vocabulary, English learners are likely to benefit from their use.

Although semantic maps are used primarily to build vocabulary and activate and organize background knowledge, teachers may facilitate aesthetic responses to the text by including a category that taps students' emotional responses to the topic, as shown in Examples 2.23 and 2.24.

Example 2.22

- **Title:** *Charlotte's Web*
- **Author:** E. B. White
- **Grade Level:** 3–5
- **Summary:** Charlotte is a clever spider who befriends a pig named Wilbur. With the help of other animals, Charlotte saves Wilbur from a sure death.

Semantic Map

Jobs

milk cows
feed animals
gather eggs
plow fields

Animals

cows
sheep
chickens
dogs
goats
pigs

FARMS

Tools & Equipment

tractors
pails
pitchforks
shovels
milking machines

Example 2.23 _____

- **Title:** *Surprising Sharks*
- **Author:** Nicola Davies
- **Grade Level:** K–3
- **Summary:** This picture book provides a wealth of information about sharks, including the numerous species of sharks, their anatomical features, and how they have more to fear from humans than humans do from them.

Semantic Map

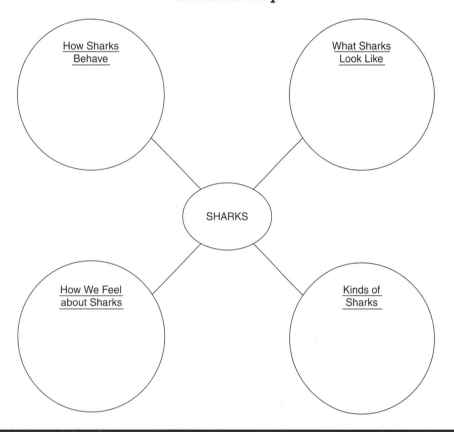

Example 2.24 _____

- **Title:** *Johnny Tremain*
- **Author:** Esther Forbes
- **Grade Level:** 5 and up
- **Summary:** When Johnny Tremain burns his hand in an accident, he can no longer serve as apprentice to a silversmith in early Boston. Instead, he delivers papers for the Sons of Liberty and becomes involved in the Revolutionary War. This book is the winner of a Newbery Medal.

Semantic Map

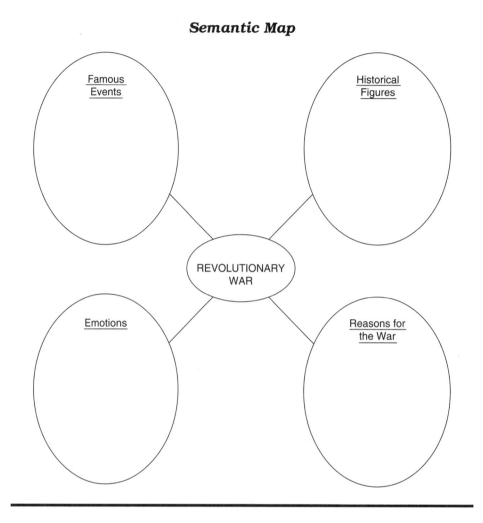

PREVIEW-PREDICT-CONFIRM

In this activity, students preview a book, make predictions about the language and content of the book, and confirm or reject their predictions after reading (Yopp & Yopp, 2004).

The activity begins with the students previewing a book by looking at each page as the teacher shares the book or by independently turning the pages of their own copies. After the students have briefly viewed each page, the teacher asks them to predict words they think the author may have used in the book without looking back at it. Three or four words are elicited, and the teacher asks for reasons the students think the words are in the book. For example, after looking at the pictures in Gail Gibbons's *Yippee-Yay!*, a book about cowboys, one student might say that he thinks the word *Texas* is in the book because cowboys live in Texas. Another student might predict the word *desert* is in the book and explain her contribution by stating that the pictures show the cowboys and cattle in the desert. A third student might explain predictions of *bandanna* and *boots* by stating that he saw a diagram in the book of cowboys' clothing that included these articles.

After several predictions are discussed, the teacher organizes the students into groups of three or four. Each group is provided with thirty to forty (or fewer, depending on the ages of the students) small blank cards and the students are asked to predict as many words as they can and to record one word on each card. Students are told not to record words unrelated to the specific content of the book (e.g., *is, the, and*).

Once the students have generated and recorded their words, they sort them into categories. Within their small groups, the students negotiate categories with one another, drawing on their observations and background knowledge to make decisions about which words fit together. Students often generate additional predictions during this opportunity to organize their words, and extra blank cards should be made available. Students label their categories and report their category labels during a quick share with the whole class.

The next step in this activity is to have each small group of students select three words from their cards: a word they think is common to all groups, a word they believe is unique to their group, and an interesting word. A representative from each group reveals his or her group's common word prediction, and the teacher notes overlap among the groups' predictions and asks why the words were chosen and what they reveal about the students' predictions about the book. What do they think the major ideas in the book will be? Next, each representative shares his or her group's unique word prediction, and, finally, each shares the group's interesting word. After each set of words is shared, the teacher asks questions about the word choices, such as, "What does the word have to do with the topic of the text?" and "In what context might the word appear?"

Finally, the students read the book or listen to it read aloud. As the book is read, students note whether their predicted words were used by the author. Whole-group or small-group discussion during or after the reading includes highlighting the author's use of predicted words, including how the words are used, as well as identifying words that might be added to categories in a group's collection. Example 2.26 shows words students thought were important to add after reading *The Moon* by Seymour Simon.

We note elsewhere that this activity supports students' comprehension in several ways (Yopp & Yopp, 2004). Foremost among them are that it contributes to vocabulary development and activates and builds relevant background knowledge as students think about words related to a topic and then semantically organize them, as students discuss words and content with peers, and as they closely attend to the words and ideas of the author. It also promotes engagement in strategic reading as students generate questions about the book and establish purposes for reading.

Participation in preview-predict-confirm before reading benefits all students, and it is particularly useful for English learners. Having illustrations serve as the focus of a preview offers students a nonverbal source of information about a text. The small-group structure provides a relatively risk-free environment for students to share their vocabulary. Students' existing vocabulary is valued and all words are accepted and considered worthy contributions. For instance, after previewing the illustrations in *Sea Turtles,* by Gail Gibbons, students may offer words that range from simpler ones such as *water* and *fish* to more sophisticated ones such as *species, reproduction,* and *endangered.* Vocabulary is clarified and elaborated on as students spontaneously offer explanations for their word choices. In addition, students expand their understanding of words as they semantically sort them.

This activity provides an excellent opportunity for the teacher to assess students' readiness for a text. If students generate very few words related to the topic of the book after previewing pictures and discussing what they saw with peers, then the teacher will need to provide instruction and experiences related to the topic prior to asking the students to read the book in order to ensure meaningful interactions with the book.

Example 2.25 _____

- **Title:** *Almost to Freedom*
- **Author:** Vaunda Micheaux Nelson
- **Grade Levels:** K–3
- **Summary:** A rag doll tells the story of her owner's escape from a Virginia plantation to freedom through the Underground Railroad. When accidentally left behind at one of the hiding places along the way, the doll is lonely until another runaway child finds it. The doll realizes it has an important job.

Preview-Predict-Confirm

Setting	People	Actions	Feelings
fire	*men*	*work*	*scared*
cotton	*mother*	*pick*	*happy*
stars	*daughter*	*arrested*	*sad*

Setting	People	Actions	Feelings
night	*father*	*watching*	*pain*
boat	*African*	*listening*	
house	*slaves*	*hide*	**Doll**
basement	*black*	*sleep*	*hold*
fields	*mouse*	*struggle*	*sew*
dark		*cry*	*hug*
ladder		*sneak*	*hold*
		row	*squeeze*
		comfort	
		climb	

Common word: *doll*

Unique word: *sew*

Interesting word: *watching*

Example 2.26

- **Title:** *The Moon*
- **Author:** Seymour Simon
- **Grade Level:** 3–6
- **Summary:** The Earth's only natural satellite, the moon is an object of great interest to scientists. The author shares information about the moon, its features and history, and the Apollo space program. Beautiful photographs accompany the informative text.

Preview-Predict-Confirm

The Moon	Studying the Moon	The Earth	Astronauts
moon	*instruments*	*Earth*	*astronaut*
craters	*rover*	*big*	*Neil Armstrong*
rock	*radio*	*small*	*spacesuit*
land	*tool*	*light*	*first*
round	*camera*	*close*	*step*
gravity	*study*		*space shuttle*
dirt	*look*	**Survival**	*footprint*
	discover	*oxygen*	
		air	
		food	
		water	
		dead	

Common word: *astronaut*

Unique word: *gravity*

Interesting word: *spacesuit*

Words Added after Reading:

different	*Apollo*	*flatlands*	*explosion*
crescent	*moonquakes*	*lava*	*feather*
old	*satellite*	*valleys*	*clover*
phases	*sun*	*mountains*	

CONCRETE EXPERIENCES

Concrete experiences support students' understanding of a text by engaging them with the objects, concepts, or events discussed in the text prior to reading about them. Concrete experiences might include observations, manipulations, or simulations. Before reading about light and shadows, for example, students might observe and record the movement of shadows on the playground. Before reading a book about simple machines, students might experiment with levers, pulleys, and inclined planes, talking about their explorations with peers in pairs or small groups. Before reading about mapmaking, students might draw their own maps of their classroom, school, or neighborhood, using the tools, skills, and language of a mapmaker.

According to Guthrie and Ozgungor (2002), concrete experiences—or real-world interactions—have both cognitive and motivational benefits. One cognitive benefit is that they cause students to activate background knowledge. As students observe, manipulate, and experience real objects and events, they often spontaneously describe prior experiences and knowledge related to the object or event and share their experiences and information with peers. When handling a collection of shells, for example, students might talk about collecting shells at the beach, share descriptions of shells they have seen, perhaps comparing them to the shells they are holding now, and discuss what they know about shells serving as homes for mollusks. This activation of background knowledge puts students in a state of readiness for new learning from text. Additional experiences with objects build background knowledge and develop vocabulary. A second cognitive benefit of concrete experiences is that they prompt students to ask questions, a strategy known to enhance comprehension (National Reading Panel, 2000; Nolte & Singer, 1985; Yopp, 1988). Questions serve as a beginning point for reading by creating a set of purposes for reading and cause students to be actively engaged with text as they read to find the answers to their questions.

Concrete experiences also have motivational benefits. Guthrie and Ozgungor (2002) argued that real-world interactions are intrinsically motivating and that the intrinsic motivation for these activities transfers to texts about the objects and experiences. Additionally, when students explore and experience real objects or events, they gain a sense of ownership over their new information. The results of students' observations and experiences become their personal knowledge, and a sense of control over one's knowledge and learning is integral to motivation (Skinner, Wellborn, & Connell, in Guthrie & Ozgungor, 2002). Any teacher who has witnessed children handling seeds, building bridges, or planning elections can appreciate the motivational aspects of these activities. This motivation carries over into reading about these experiences.

The use of concrete experiences is particularly supportive of English learners and is often recommended by authorities in second-language learning (Peregoy & Boyle, 2005). Use of realia supports students' efforts to learn new content because it provides something tangible to support their meaning making. Additionally, concrete experiences prompt purposeful and informal conversations in a low-anxiety setting, so English learners are more likely to engage in discussions. Indeed, all students make use of or begin developing relevant vocabulary as they talk with one another about what they are observing or experiencing.

Concrete experiences can be provided for many texts the students read and are especially appropriate for informational text. In the examples that follow, teachers provide students with opportunities to observe, touch, manipulate, and experience real objects and discuss their experiences with peers prior to sharing related texts with them.

Example 2.27 _____

- **Title:** *Pop! A Book about Bubbles*
- **Author:** Kimberly Brubaker Bradley
- **Grade Level:** K–3
- **Summary:** What are bubbles? Are they always round? How can you make bubbles? Why do they pop? These and many other questions are answered in this book about bubbles.

Concrete Experiences

1. Have the students make a bubble solution. (A recipe is provided in the book.)
2. Provide bubble wands and allow the students to experiment freely with the solution.
3. After some free exploration, suggest that the students trying blowing slowly and quickly into their bubble wands and waving their wands in the air. Discuss what they observe.
4. Ask the students to describe bubbles. What is their shape? Can the students make other shapes? Do they see any bubbles that are attached to each other or other objects? What do they look like?
5. Ask the students what happens when they touch a bubble. What happens to a bubble if they do not touch it?
6. Ask the students where they have seen bubbles. Show them bubbles in a glass of soda, and ask them to describe what they see.
7. Ask volunteers to blow bubbles through a straw into various liquids, such as water, milk, and soda. What do they observe? Why do they think there might be differences?

Example 2.28 _____

- **Title:** *A Drop of Water*
- **Author:** Walter Wick
- **Grade Level:** 3–6
- **Summary:** Beautiful photography supports the text in this informational book about water. Topics include surface tension, adhesion, capillary attraction, evaporation, condensation, and others.

Concrete Experiences

The teacher can engage students in a variety of experiences that will support their understandings of the concepts in this book. We suggest three activities here, and others are provided by the author at the end of the book. After participating in several experiences, the teacher may want to ask the students to think about observations of water they have made outside of the classroom, particularly as they illustrate the phenomena demonstrated in the activities below. Or, the teacher may write the word *water* in the middle of the board or chart paper and have the students create a cluster of what they know about water and questions they have about water.

1. *Water Drops on a Penny Activity:* Provide each pair of students with a penny, a cup of water, and an eye dropper. Ask the students to predict how many drops of water will fit on top of the penny, and then allow them to conduct tests and record their findings. They should see the water build up on top of the penny until the surface tension finally breaks, causing the water to spill over. When discussing the student's observations, use the terms *cohesion* and *surface tension* to describe these properties of water. (*Cohesion* is the attraction of water molecules to each other. *Surface tension* is the cohesion of water molecules at the surface of a body of water.) Encourage questions and explorations. How many drops might fit on a nickel or a quarter? Does it matter whether the students hold the eye dropper above the water collecting on top of the penny or touch the water with the tip of the eye dropper? Do other liquids have this same property?

2. *Joining Water Drops Activity:* Have the students draw circles on a piece of paper and tape the paper to a hard flat surface that can be picked up and moved, such as a lapboard. Have the students tape waxed paper over the drawing. Ask the students to use an eye dropper to place two or three drops of water in each circle and then to tilt the lapboard to move the drops of water so they connect to each other and become one drop of water. What did the students observe? Was it easy or difficult to move the droplets across the surface? Discuss their observations, using the terms *cohesion* and *adhesion* to identify the processes of a substance attaching to itself and attaching to something else, respectively.

3. *Capillary Attraction Activity:* Have the students place a drop of water on a dry plate and hold a paper towel over the plate so that a corner of the towel barely touches the water drop. Ask the students to observe what happens. They should see water "climb" up the paper towel. This phenomenon is called capillary attraction or capillary action. Invite the students to talk about what they see.

PICTURE PACKETS

Similar to concrete experiences are experiences with photographs, drawings, graphics, and other visual information relevant to a reading selection. Before reading, packets containing visuals that have been downloaded from the Internet, cut from newspapers and magazines, or obtained from other sources are given to students to examine and discuss with peers. For example, before reading *Probing Volcanoes,* by Laurie Lindop, small groups of students study photographs of dormant and active volcanoes, volcanic ash and rock, and volcanic craters. Students talk about what they know about volcanoes and what they see in the pictures, negotiating meaning and clarifying ideas. They generate questions about volcanoes, thus setting personal purposes for reading. Before reading *Out of the Dust,* by Karen Hesse, students handle photographs of the Dust Bowl, weather charts, and maps of the region. Students have both affective and cognitive reactions as they see dust piled four feet deep against a house, devastated farmland, and blackened skies.

Dragon's Gate, by Lawrence Yep, is a fictional account of Chinese immigrants' roles in building the transcontinental railroad. Before reading, students examine visuals such as photographs of Chinese laborers and the conditions in which they lived, the ships on which the laborers traveled, the blasting of tunnels in mountainsides, and the driving of the Golden Spike; charts of the numbers of Chinese and other laborers; copies of newspaper articles; and maps detailing the route of the railroad. With access to the World Wide Web, teachers can readily locate visuals to share with students. Multiple packets should be made so that every small group of students has access and can closely view the materials. Alternatively, students themselves may search the Internet for visuals related to a topic and share them with peers.

As students view the materials, they think about what the visuals reveal about the topic and what feelings they evoke. The teacher might ask the students to sort the materials in some way that makes sense to them, or the teacher might lead the students in constructing a K-W-L chart or a semantic map about the topic of the book.

The use of visuals builds and activates students' background knowledge, arouses their curiosity, and stimulates personal reactions to the content. The visuals provide a nonverbal source of information, providing comprehensible input for English learners. At the same time, the peer group and teacher-facilitated discussions are instrumental in building learners' background knowledge and their academic language.

QUICKWRITES FROM EXPERIENCE AND SPEEDWRITING

Quickwrites from experience (QWE) and speedwriting (Luse, 2002) serve to promote personal connections between the reader and the text, activate students' existing knowledge, and stimulate thinking on a topic prior to students' encounters with a reading selection.

When students are likely to have had personal experiences that provide background knowledge relevant to the subject of a text, QWE is useful. Given a prompt from the teacher, participants in QWE recall and quickly write about an experience. For example, before reading *Throw Your Tooth on the Roof,* by Selby B. Beeler, students think about their own experiences in losing baby teeth. What became of the baby teeth? Many cultures have traditions surrounding the loss of a baby tooth: It is put under a pillow, buried in a garden, dropped down a mouse hole, or thrown on a roof. Beeler's book describes traditions from cultures around the world. Thinking and writing about their own experiences with lost teeth prior to reading stimulates students' personal connections with the topic.

Likewise, before reading about a Chinese American's wishes for his birthday in *Happy Birthday Mr. Kang*, by Susan L. Roth, students reflect on and write about wishes they have had for their own birthdays. Before reading about a young girl who has an unusual name in Kevin Henkes's *Chrysanthemum*, students briefly write something about their own name: its origin, their feelings about their name, or an incident involving their name.

After writing, students are provided an opportunity to share—in pairs, small groups, or as a class—their writing with peers. Conversations about the topic ensue and students may question one another for more detail, particularly as diverse responses are given. Example 2.29 provides sample QWEs about waking up in the morning.

Example 2.29

- **Title:** *Mary Smith*
- **Author:** Andrea U'Ren
- **Grade Level:** 1–3
- **Summary:** Years ago, before the time when alarm clocks were common, people hired "knockers up" to awaken them in the morning. Most knockers up carried long poles and scratched on the windows of their clients' homes. Mary Smith used a peashooter to shoot dried peas at their windows.

Quickwrites from Experience

Prompt: Take a few minutes to write about how you are awakened from sleep, especially on mornings when you need to rise early. What awakens you from your sleep?

Student 1:

My mom has an alarm clock. Usually I hear it go off while I sleep, but I roll over and keep sleeping until my mother jiggles my arm and tells me it is time to get up. Sometimes she has to come back three or four times to get me out of bed. When that happens she grabs my feet and tosses them over the side of the bed and pulls me into a standing position. Sometimes when I'm anxious about something the night before, I automatically wake up early the next morning.

Student 2:

Usually my parents wake me up. Sometimes I hear my brothers talking in their room and that wakes me up. Some mornings when I want to be sure to get up early I leave the blinds on my windows open so that the sun shines through them in the morning. The way my room faces, the sun really makes my room light and that usually wakes me up.

Student 3:

My dog always sleeps with me. She usually wakes me up early in the morning because she wants to play and to be let outside. She whimpers and puts her nose right in my face. My dog is like my alarm clock.

When students are unlikely to have had personal experiences related to the content of a reading selection, they may engage instead in speed-writing (Luse, 2002) in which they write in one minute as much as they can about a topic. For example, before reading *By the Great Horn Spoon!*, by Sid Fleischman, students write what they know about the California Gold Rush, the setting of Fleischman's story. Before reading *Baseball Saved Us*, by Ken Mochizuki, they write what they know about the Japanese American experience during World War II. If students are unable to think of anything to write, they record what they want to know or they list questions. Luse has suggested that students count their words when time is called and that they try to increase the number of words they write in each speed-writing session, even though the topics may differ. Students share their ideas with one another and engage in conversations about what they know (or think they know) about the topic. The same prompt may be given after students engage with a reading selection and students may check to see if their list has increased or been modified. Example 2.30 shares a list generated by a sixth-grader on the topic of humankind's first landing on the moon.

Example 2.30

- **Title:** *The Man Who Went to the Far Side of the Moon: The Story of Apollo 11 Astronaut Michael Collins*
- **Author:** Bee Uusma Schyffert
- **Grade Level:** 4–8
- **Summary:** This book, a biography of Michael Collins, who remained in orbit around the moon while his fellow astronauts landed on the moon in 1969, offers a close look at an exhilarating event in humankind's history. Interesting information that captures the imagination of readers is shared in a variety of text formats.

Speedwriting

Prompt: In one minute, write everything you know about our first lunar landing.

Student Response:

The United States was first to put a person on the moon.

There were three astronauts.

The first man said, "One small step for man, one giant leap for mankind."

The first person on the moon left a flag and footprints.

Neil Armstrong was the first man on the moon.

We landed on the moon in the 1960s.

Quickwrites from experience and speedwriting stimulate thinking about the topic of a text as students reflect on what they have experienced or what they know about the topic prior to reading. During QWE, students draw on their personal experiences, and during speedwriting, they draw on their knowledge of a topic. In both cases, background knowledge is activated and personal connections are made as students reflect on their own experiences and knowledge and learn from the experiences and knowledge of one another.

In these prereading activities, as in many, students discover that what they have experienced and what they already know matter in the reading act. Further, they appreciate that the contributions of all students are important and valuable. The more diverse the student population, the richer the pool of experiences and information that will be shared.

English learners may be encouraged to record their thoughts in the language that is most comfortable for them. If students are writing in a less familiar language, they should be given ample time to write. The time limit that Luse (2002) suggested for speedwriting, then, must be considered with caution by teachers. Further, teachers may want to provide all students with a moment of quiet reflection, or think time, prior to writing.

QUICKDRAWS

Quickdraws provide a different medium for students to reflect on and share their experiences or knowledge. Although appropriate for use with all students, quickdraws can be particularly effective with students who are new to the English language and students who are developing as users of written language.

Students are asked to quickly develop a sketch in response to a prompt. For instance, a teacher might provide students with a few minutes to quickly draw what they know about how electricity gets to their homes prior to sharing Barbara Seuling's *Flick a Switch: How Electricity Gets to Your Home.* Some children might draw electrical outlets, wires running through walls, and utility poles; others might draw transformers, electrical grids, wind turbines, dams, and nuclear power plants. After drawing, students are given the opportunity to talk about their drawings with one another. They are encouraged to revise or elaborate on their drawings based on their conversations with peers. Students are also encouraged to generate questions as they engage in drawing and discussing. The teacher records students' questions on an overhead transparency or chart.

Example 2.31 shares one student's drawings of the front and back of a dollar bill before reading about the meaning of the symbols on U.S. currency. After the students drew from memory, they shared their drawings with peers and then refined their drawings. Then, the teacher shared several dollar bills for students to examine closely. Included in the example are some of the questions that students generated.

Quickdraws provide an opportunity for teachers to learn about students' experiences with a topic, their existing knowledge on that topic, and misconceptions they may have.

Example 2.31 _____

- **Title:** *Money, Money, Money*
- **Author:** Nancy Winslow Parker
- **Grade Level:** 3–6

■ **Summary:** The author provides interesting information about the meaning of the symbols and art on the paper currency of the United States. Readers also will learn about the individuals whose pictures are on the bills, the engraving and printing process, counterfeiting, and more.

Quickdraws from Experience

Prompt: You probably handle or see money every day. In as much detail as possible, draw the front and back of a one-dollar bill without looking at one.

These questions were generated by the students after drawing, discussing, and viewing a dollar bill:

Whose pictures are put on the paper money?

Why is there a pyramid?

What does the eye represent?

Why do some bills have an asterisk in the row of numbers?

Why is there more than one language on the bill?

What do those foreign words mean?

Why is there a city name on the bill?

What is the largest bill?

How is money made?

Why is the eagle holding arrows in its talons?

CONCLUSION

The twelve prereading activities described in this chapter set the stage for personal responses to the literature, activate or build background knowledge, develop relevant language, prompt students to set purposes for reading, and motivate students to read. The activities involve students in thinking, discussing, responding, exploring, and shaping ideas. Students are likely to find the literature personally meaningful after engaging in these activities and to approach ideas contained in the books with greater interest, purpose, involvement, and appreciation.

REFERENCES

Babbitt, N. (1975). *Tuck everlasting.* New York: Farrar, Straus & Giroux.

Beeler, S. B. (1998). *Throw your tooth on the roof.* Boston: Houghton Mifflin.

Bradley, K. B. (2001). *Pop! A book about bubbles.* New York: HarperTrophy.

Brinckloe, J. (1985). *Fireflies!* New York: Aladdin.

Bruchac, J. (1993). *The first strawberries.* New York: Penguin Puffin.

Clements, A. (2002). *Things not seen.* New York: Philomel.

Creech, S. (2001). *A fine, fine school.* New York: HarperCollins.

Davies, N. (2003). *Surprising sharks.* Cambridge, MA: Candlewick.

Ets, M. H. (1963). *Gilberto and the wind.* New York: Scholastic.

Farmer, J. (1999). *Bananas!* Watertown, MA: Charlesbridge.

Farnan, N., Flood, J., & Lapp, D. (1994). Comprehending through reading and writing: Six research-based instructional strategies. In K. Spangenberg-Urbschat & R. Pritchard (Eds.), *Kids come in all languages: Reading instruction for ESL* (pp. 135–157). Newark, DE: International Reading Association.

Fleischman, P. (1988). *Joyful noise.* New York: HarperTrophy.

Fleischman, S. (1963). *By the great horn spoon!* Boston: Little, Brown.

Fletcher, R. (1998). *Flying solo.* New York: Clarion.

Forbes, E. (1971). *Johnny Tremain.* New York: Dell.

Gibbons, G. (1995). *Sea turtles.* New York: Holiday House.

Gibbons, G. (1998). *Marshes & swamps.* New York: Holiday House.

Gibbons, G. (1998). *Yippee-yay!* New York: Little, Brown.

Golenbock, P. (1990). *Teammates.* San Diego, CA: Harcourt Brace.

Guthrie, J. T., & Ozgungor, S. (2002). Instructional contexts for reading engagement. In C. C. Block & M. Pressley (Eds.), *Comprehension instruction: Research-based best practices* (pp. 275–288). New York: Guilford.

Henkes, K. (1991). *Chrysanthemum.* New York: Greenwillow.

Hesse, K. (1999). *Out of the dust.* New York: Scholastic.

Horvath, P. (1991). *Everything on a waffle.* New York: Scholastic.

Johnson, D., & Pearson, P. D. (1984). *Teaching reading vocabulary* (2nd ed.). New York: Holt, Rinehart, & Winston.

Johnson, D., Pittelman, S., & Heimlich, J. (1986). Semantic mapping. *The Reading Teacher, 39,* 778–783.

Lindop, L. (2003). *Probing volcanoes.* Fairfield, IA: 21st Century Books.

Luse, P. L. (2002). Speedwriting: A teaching strategy for active student engagement. *The Reading Teacher, 56,* 20–29.

Mandeville, T. F. (1994). KWLA: Linking the affective and cognitive domains. *The Reading Teacher, 47,* 679–680.

McNeil, J. (1987). *Reading comprehension: New directions for classroom practice* (2nd ed.). Glenview, IL: Scott, Foresman.

Mochizuki, K. (1993). *Baseball saved us.* New York: Lee & Low.

Murphy, J. (2003). *An American plague: The true and terrifying story of the yellow fever epidemic of 1793.* New York: Clarion.

National Reading Panel. (2000). *Teaching children to read: An evidence-based assessment of scientific research literature on reading and its implications for reading instruction* (NIH Publication No. 00-4769). Washington, DC: U.S. Government Printing Office.

Nelson, V. M. (2003). *Almost to freedom.* Minneapolis: Carolrhoda.

Nolte, R. Y., & Singer, H. (1985). Active comprehension: Teaching a process of reading comprehension and its effects on reading achievement. *The Reading Teacher, 39,* 24–31.

O'Dell, S. (1960). *Island of the Blue Dolphins.* New York: Houghton Miffin.

Ogle, D. (1986). K-W-L: A teaching model that develops active reading of expository text. *The Reading Teacher, 39,* 564–570.

Parker, N. W. (1995). *Money, money, money.* New York: HarperCollins.

Paterson, K. *The great Gilly Hopkins.* New York: HarperTrophy.

Peregoy, S. F., & Boyle, O. F. (2005). *Reading, writing, and learning in ESL.* Boston: Pearson.

Polacco, P. (1990). *Thunder cake.* New York: Philomel.

Rathman, P. (1995). *Officer Buckle and Gloria.* New York: Scholastic.

Rawls, W. (1961). *Where the red fern grows.* New York: Doubleday.

Readence, J., Bean, T., & Baldwin, R. (1981). *Content area reading: An integrated approach.* Dubuque, IA: Kendall/Hunt.

Reasoner, C. F. (1976). *Releasing children to literature* (rev. ed.). New York: Dell.

Roth, S. L. (2001). *Happy birthday Mr. Kang.* Washington, DC: National Geographic.

Sachar, L. (1998). *Holes.* New York: Farrar, Straus & Giroux.

Schyffert, B. U. (2003 translation). *The man who went to the far side of the moon.* San Francisco: Chronicle.

Seuling, B. (2003). *Flick a switch: How electricity gets to your home.* New York: Holiday House.

Simon, S. (2003). *The moon.* New York: Simon & Schuster.

Sinatra, R., Stahi-Gemake, J., & Berg, D. (1984). Improving reading comprehension of disabled readers through semantic mapping. *The Reading Teacher, 38,* 22–29.

Sorensen, V. (1957). *Miracles on Maple Hill.* New York: Harcourt Brace & World.

Spinelli, J. (2002). *Stargirl.* New York: Knopf.

Stahl, S., & Vancil, S. (1986). Discussion is what makes semantic maps work in vocabulary instruction. *The Reading Teacher, 40,* 62–67.

Taba, H. (1967). *Teachers handbook for elementary social studies.* Reading, MA: Addison-Wesley.

Taylor, M. (1983). *Roll of thunder, hear my cry.* Toronto: Bantam.

U'Ren, A. (2003). *Mary Smith.* New York: Farrar, Straus & Giroux.

Viorst, J. (1972). *Alexander and the terrible, horrible, no good, very bad day.* New York: Atheneum.

White, E. B. (1973). *Stuart Little.* New York: Harper & Row.

White, E. B. (1974). *Charlotte's web.* New York: HarperTrophy.

Wick, W. (1997). *A drop of water.* New York: Scholastic.

Yep, L. (1975). *Dragonwings.* New York: Harper Junior Books.

Yep, L. (1995). *Dragon's gate.* New York: HarperTrophy.

Yopp, R. H. (1988). Questioning and active comprehension. *Questioning Exchange, 2,* 231–238.

Yopp, R. H., & Yopp, H. K. (2004). Preview-predict-confirm: Thinking about the language and content of informational text. *The Reading Teacher, 58,* 79–83.

CHAPTER THREE

During-Reading Activities

During Reading

Purposes

- To prompt students' use of comprehension strategies
- To enhance awareness and use of text structures
- To focus attention on language
- To facilitate thinking about characters, events, themes, and big ideas
- To promote collaborative building of interpretations
- To allow for personal responses

Activities

- Literature circles
- Literature maps
- Character maps
- Character webs
- Graphic organizers
- Character perspective charts
- Journals
- Feelings charts
- Contrast charts
- Ten important words

There will be many occasions when teachers introduce a book and the students read it uninterrupted. During some literature experiences, however, teachers may choose to engage students in activities that facilitate and deepen comprehension of a selection and encourage personal responses to the literature.

Without comprehension, reading has not occurred and literature is of no value. Students' eyes may trail across lines of text, students may pronounce the words on the page, and they may even be able to tell us that Little Red Riding Hood's cape is red, but we cannot say they have read a selection unless they have constructed understandings of the selection. To read is to make meaning. Much of what students do before reading prepares them for meaningful interactions with the text. It is during reading, however, that students must actively engage with a text to build their understandings of it.

As we note in Chapter One, activities that prompt students' use of comprehension strategies—such as generating questions, creating visual images, summarizing, and making connections between their background knowledge and experiences and the text—enhance students' comprehension. Likewise, activities that guide students to notice and make use of text structures; focus their attention on the author's language; facilitate their thinking about characters, events, themes, and big ideas in the selection; and promote their collaborative building of interpretations of text with peers support comprehension. As students read and revisit sections of a selection and engage in during-reading activities, they actively process text.

During-reading activities also play a significant role in encouraging students' personal responses to literature. Although an efferent stance wherein students carry away information from a reading selection is important, literature is most powerful and most memorable when students approach it from an aesthetic stance. One way to promote an aesthetic stance is to provide an environment in which students are encouraged to respond personally to works of literature and to explore the responses of their classmates. During-reading activities that invite students to bring themselves to the literary experience, listen to the points of view of others, reflect on their own responses, and make connections between their lives and ideas in the text are critical to supporting aesthetic stances to reading.

This chapter describes ten activities in which teachers may engage students during reading to deepen their understandings and responses to literature. *Literature circles* encourage students' strategic reading, negotiation of meaning with peers, and personal responses. *Literature maps* enhance students' comprehension by assisting them in identifying and organizing information they find important or interesting. Literature maps can be used to focus students' attention on text elements, such as setting and characters; to call attention to language; and to allow for personal responses. *Character maps* are used for analyzing characters and their evolving relationships. *Character webs* also may be used to analyze characters. They differ from character maps in that the students record evidence from the text to support identified character traits. *Graphic organizers* support students' understanding of text structures and content. *Character perspective charts* prompt students to think about story elements from more than one point of view. Several *journal* formats are described in this chapter, all of which promote reactions and personal responses to reading selections. *Feelings charts* provide a format for identifying and describing different viewpoints. *Contrast charts,* described in Chapter Two as a prereading activity, are appropriate for all phases of the instructional cycle, and they are included here so the reader may see examples of their application in another context and therefore gain a greater appreciation of their flexibility. The *ten important words* activity supports students' thoughtful interactions with text as they identify key words that capture the essence of a selection and build summaries of the content.

Thus, the during-reading activities in this chapter are offered with the following purposes in mind:

- To prompt students' use of comprehension strategies
- To enhance awareness and use of text structures
- To focus attention on language
- To facilitate thinking about characters, events, themes, and big ideas
- To promote collaborative building of interpretations
- To prompt personal responses

All students can benefit from participation in these activities. Very capable students will appreciate opportunities for divergent thinking, critical examination of text, making connections to their own lives, identifying what they find most interesting in the text, and directing their own interactions with the text as they, for example, generate questions, lead discussions, or select important words and ideas. Lower-achieving readers, too, will find helpful the opportunities to negotiate meaning with peers, think about and make use of text structures to organize text content, examine text for evidence supporting their interpretations, use comprehension strategies for authentic reasons, and make connections between their lives and the text.

English learners will reap the benefits of participation in these activities for many of the same reasons. In addition, the use of graphics in some of these activities and the social interactions that are the heart of the activities when well used will support English learners' understandings. Because social interactions focus on communication, students' language is supported as they work to clarify ideas. At the same time, because some of these activities draw attention to the rich language that literature offers, English learners will have opportunities for building academic language proficiency.

LITERATURE CIRCLES

Literature circles are temporary groupings of four or five students who meet regularly to discuss a work of literature that all members of the group have chosen to read. Each group decides when and how long to meet and how much of the selection to read between meetings. Group members assign themselves specific responsibilities for each upcoming discussion. These responsibilities are rotated. When a group has completed the book, it decides whether and how to share it with the entire class. Then the group is disbanded.

Daniels (1994) has provided several suggestions for group member responsibilities. Students may choose from among these, or the teacher may narrow the choices based on the text and students' needs. One responsibility is to serve as Discussion Director. This student generates discussion questions based on the reading and leads the discussion when the group meets. The Literary Luminary (for works of fiction) and Passage Master (for nonfiction) locate three or four brief passages to read aloud and respond to with the group. Choices may include interesting descriptions, humorous events, or important information; any reason for selecting a passage is acceptable. The Illustrator draws a picture or diagram that is related to the text. The Connector makes connections between the text and his or her own personal life, school life, events in the community, other writings, or anything else that the Connector feels is appropriate. The Vocabulary Enricher selects vocabulary from the text to share. Vocabulary choices may include unknown words, powerful words or phrases, or words that the author uses in an interesting way. The Travel Tracer's job is to record the movements of a character in the portion of text under discussion. This student writes a description or draws a map of a character's travels. The Investigator locates information that is relevant to the reading. This may be information, for instance, about the author, the setting, or the time period.

Examples 3.1, 3.2, 3.3, and 3.4 show the notes of two Discussion Directors, a Connector, and a Vocabulary Enhancer for four different groups. These notes are not turned in to the group but, rather, are used to support the discussion.

Literature circles are useful for promoting students' responses to literature. By taking on a variety of roles in these groups, students develop appreciation for the multifaceted ways one might respond to a text. Students take ownership of their reading and the discussions and share what is meaningful to them. The literature circle experience allows students to make decisions about their reading, actively engage with the text and peers, explore ideas, and build and revise their understandings of the literature.

Further, the peer interaction that occurs in literature circles increases opportunities for meaningful communication using academic language, thus supporting English learners' oral language development. Additionally, literature circles provide a social learning context in which peers' scaffolding and modeling help students internalize and imitate literacy behaviors as they negotiate meaning and express their comprehension.

Example 3.1

- **Title:** *Mr. Popper's Penguins*
- **Author:** Richard and Florence Atwater
- **Grade Level:** 3–5
- **Summary:** Mr. Popper receives a penguin in the mail after sending a letter to an Arctic scientist. Mr. Popper and the penguin, named Captain Cook, have a number of hilarious adventures until the penguin's loneliness results in declining health. Soon Captain Cook is sent a mate, Greta, and nature takes its course, resulting in a house full of penguins. Mr. Popper takes the penguins on the road to perform their antics for audiences everywhere. Eventually, he makes the difficult decision to return the penguins to their natural habitat—and he accompanies them.

Discussion Director
(Chapters 8–9)

What were these chapters about?

What would you think if you were getting your hair cut and someone came in with a penguin?

What do you think will happen now that Greta is there?

What would you do if you had a pet that became mopey?

Do you think Mr. Popper and Captain Cook will get into more trouble?

Example 3.2

- **Title:** *Olive's Ocean*
- **Author:** Kevin Henkes
- **Grade Level:** 5–8
- **Summary:** Martha did not know Olive well, so she was surprised when Olive's mother gave her a page from Olive's journal after the girl was killed in a bicycle accident. Martha learns from the journal entry that she and Olive had similar interests and that Olive had hoped they would become friends. Martha can't stop thinking about Olive while on a family visit to Cape Cod where she, on the brink of adolescence, learns much about herself and life.

Discussion Director
(Chapters 1–5)

What do you think about how the author opened this book?

Have you ever been surprised to find out what someone is thinking about you?

How would you react to Olive's mother if you were Martha?

Do you think Martha will tell her parents about the journal page and her feelings?

Why did Martha visit the place where Olive died? Why do you think she wrote Olive's name and left a bracelet there?

Example 3.3

- **Title:** *Island of the Blue Dolphins*
- **Author:** Scott O'Dell
- **Grade Level:** 4–6
- **Summary:** Living on an island off the coast of California, Karana's people choose to abandon their island after many of the men are killed. Just as the ship is departing the island, Karana sees her brother left behind and leaps off the boat to stay with him. Karana soon finds herself alone when her brother is killed by wild dogs. Karana's story of survival on the island for 18 years and her friendship with Rontu, a dog, is a children's classic.

Connector
(Chapters 17–18)

Text: *I can relate this book to* Because of Winn-Dixie *because in both stories a dog comes into a human's life and keeps her company and helps her. In each book, the dog is a very special companion.*

Self: *I can connect this story to me because I have a dog and it just popped into my life just like in the two stories. For years I wanted a dog and then one day, with no planning, one joined my family. It was an unexpected and wonderful addition to our family. I think I feel about my dog the way Opal immediately felt about Winn-Dixie and Karana eventually felt about Rontu.*

World: *I can connect this book to the world because many people face difficult and sad times but they can still find joy in life. In spite of hardships in their lives, both Opal and Karana find things to be thankful for.*

Example 3.4

- **Title:** *Bearstone*
- **Author:** Will Hobbs
- **Grade Level:** 5–8
- **Summary:** This Notable Children's Trade Book in the Field of Social Studies is another of Will Hobbs's coming-of-age stories of resilience and survival. Constantly in trouble, parentless fourteen-year-old Cloyd has been sent by his tribe to live with an old rancher in the Colorado mountains. There, he learns about life, love, and himself.

Vocabulary Enricher
(Chapter 4)

I picked four words because I wasn't sure what they meant.

admonish

Pages 18–19: "Old friends who dropped by would admonish *him for not keeping up his strength, but as he told them, he was never hungry."*

According to the dictionary, admonish *means to caution, scold, or urge. I think here it means that his friends scolded him.*

devoid

Page 19: "Cloyd's large, round face was devoid *of expression, unless it was the mouth turning dourly down at the corners."*

The dictionary says that devoid *means totally lacking. Cloyd had no expression on his face. His face was blank (except for his mouth).*

dourly

Page 19: "Cloyd's large, round face was devoid of expression, unless it was the mouth turning dourly *down at the corners."*

Dour *means sullen (bad humor, resentment), gloomy, or stern. Cloyd's frown makes it look like he's in a bad mood.*

potsherds

Page 21: "Well, they say they lived all along the river—I've found a few grinding stones and whatnot, a few arrowheads and some potsherds.*"*

Potsherds *are broken pottery fragments. The broken pottery and arrowheads are evidence that Indians did live along the river.*

LITERATURE MAPS

Literature maps, described by Haskell (1987), provide a means for responding to literature while reading. Literature maps are constructed by folding a piece of paper (8½-by-11-inch or larger) into four or more sections and labeling each section with a category name. Categories may include "setting," "themes," "predictions," "vocabulary," "questions," "symbols," "imagery," "reactions," or the names of characters. Categories are generally identified by the teacher. However, some students may like to create their own categories as they are reading.

The reader's task is to write category-related information in each section as he or she reads a chapter or a book. For example, given a section labeled "setting," the reader jots down words, phrases, or sentences about the setting of the story. It is not necessary for the student to record all data relevant to a particular category. Rather, each student includes what he or she considers the most interesting or important information. A category such as "language" will yield diverse responses from students. Some students will write expressions they think are funny or unusual. Others may record words or phrases that confuse them. Still others may write descriptive phrases. As children bring their individuality to the literature, they will respond differently from one another.

Once the maps have been completed by individual students, they are shared. The teacher or group recorder draws a large map on a piece of butcher paper and asks the group members to contribute responses from their personal maps to the group map. Students may modify their personal maps while creating the group map.

As Haskell (1987) pointed out, the benefits of this activity are many. First, students become more actively involved in their reading. They paraphrase ideas and identify important or interesting information while they are reading. Second, discussion is enhanced. Because children have taken notes while reading, they are better prepared to discuss the traits or behaviors of a particular character, for example. Third, the students have a record to which they may refer when writing about the reading selection. Fourth, students have the opportunity to hear what their peers think is important or interesting. Fifth, students begin to notice language that is appealing or effective. They begin to comment, "I like the way the author described that"—a first step toward internalizing and modeling effective language. Sixth, a map may be constructed at several points in a book, and students can trace the development of the plot or of characters.

An additional and very important benefit of this activity is that all students can contribute to a group map and feel success as their ideas are included. For example, given a particular character, some students may simply respond with physical characteristics such as "has red hair" or "is five years old," while other students may generate higher-level responses such as "is considerate of others," "is a listener," or "appears to have a good self-concept." All responses should be recorded. Thus, all students will feel comfortable responding and should have something to contribute to the group map and follow-up discussion. When a higher-level response is given, the teacher should ask, "What makes you think so?" The student then must draw on incidents from the reading selection that led to his or her conclusions. By verbalizing his or her reasons, the student is making his or her thinking overt.

It is important that the teacher avoid overwhelming the students with too many categories. Further, the teacher must recognize that some students may find this activity disruptive to their reading, particularly if they feel the need to stop quite frequently to record information. We recommend that students who find this activity disruptive be allowed to listen to or read a selection in its entirety first, then complete the literature map during a second reading. Or, students may mark pages containing information related to literature map topics with self-adhesive paper. They return to these pages later to complete their literature maps.

Example 3.5

- **Title:** *Ramona and Her Father*
- **Author:** Beverly Cleary
- **Grade Level:** 3–5
- **Summary:** Ramona's father loses his job, Ramona and Beezus go on a campaign to help him quit smoking, and Ramona practices acting so she can get a job on television commercials and earn enough money to help support her family.

Literature Map

Ramona	*Her Father*
happy	*lost his job*
making Christmas list	*worried*
loves gummy bears	*no fun anymore*
wants to help family	*patient*
practices commercials	*no money*
gets burs in hair	
Beezus	*Questions*
grouchy	*Will her father get another job?*
loves gummy bears	*Will her father be fun again?*
going through a phase	*Will Ramona be in commercials?*

Literature maps are useful at any grade level. A kindergarten teacher may modify the activity by leading a discussion and serving as recorder on a group map. The teacher may wish to read the book aloud in its entirety first. Then upon rereading, the teacher may ask students to listen for particular information in order to construct a literature map. Students may be asked to pay attention to the traits and actions of certain characters or to the setting, for instance. The teacher records students' ideas under these topics on the map. The teacher may ask students to identify what they are thinking or feeling at particular points in the story. These comments are included in a "Reactions" category.

Example 3.6

- **Title:** *Are You My Mother?*
- **Author:** P. D. Eastman
- **Grade Level:** K–1
- **Summary:** A little bird breaks out of his shell while his mother is away searching for food. The baby bird sets off to find his mother and asks a variety of animals and vehicles if they are his mother before he is reunited with her.

Literature Map

Mother Bird		**Baby Bird**	
cares about her baby		*breaks out of shell*	
goes off to find food		*leaves nest and falls*	
		can't fly	
		wants to find his mother	
Possible Mothers		**Questions**	
kitten	*steam shovel*	*Will the baby bird find his mother?*	
hen	*plane*	*Will the baby bird get hurt?*	
dog	*boat*	*Will the baby bird get lost?*	
cow	*car*		

Example 3.7

- **Title:** *Hoot*
- **Author:** Carl Hiaasen
- **Grade Level:** 5–8
- **Summary:** Roy Eberhardt's curiosity leads him to befriend a homeless boy and his sister and save some endangered owls from the proposed construction of a Mother Paula's All-American Pancake House. In the process, he learns to accept his new life in Florida.

Literature Map
(Chapters 1–2)

Roy Eberhardt	Curly
middle school student	*bald*
victim of bully on school bus	*cranky and gruff*
curious about running boy	*upset about vandalism ruining construction schedule*
new at school	*supervising engineer at construction site*
moves a lot because his dad works for the government	*pretends he doesn't see owls*
angry about moving	

Events	Questions and Predictions
Roy sees running boy from bus while Dana is squeezing his head.	*Who is the running boy?*
Curly reports vandalism on construction site to Officer Delinko.	*Why is Roy so curious?*
Roy sees the boy again, hits Dana, and jumps off the bus to chase the running boy.	*Why isn't Roy more upset about how Dana treats him?*
Roy gets injured by a golf ball.	*I think that Roy will skip school to find the running boy.*
He gets in trouble with the vice principal for hitting Dana.	*Who is the girl and why does she tell Roy to mind his own business?*

Setting	Interesting Language
school bus	*A bald man is named Curly.*
construction site	*"cowgirl"*
Trace Middle School	*"whassamatter"*
neighborhood	
golf course	

Example 3.8 _____

- **Title:** *Because of Winn-Dixie*
- **Author:** Katie DiCamillo
- **Grade Level:** 3–6
- **Summary:** When ten-year-old Opal and her father move to Florida, Opal is lonely until she unexpectedly becomes the owner of a big friendly dog. Because of the dog, Winn-Dixie, Opal meets and befriends a number of interesting people in her new town. She begins to accept that her mother, who left the family when Opal was age three, may never return, and Opal and her father find that the world still contains some happiness.

Literature Map
(Chapters 6–7)

Setting	Opal
Herman W. Block Memorial Library old house full of books windows low enough for a dog to look in Florida Years ago— Palmetto trees and big mosquitoes wild bears in the area	cares about other people likes books talks easily with adults thinks a lot about her mother

Winn-Dixie	Miss Franny
doesn't like to be left alone scares Miss Franny a people dog sensitive to people's feelings smiles talented	librarian Opal's first friend in Naomi, Florida very small, very old Herman W. Block's daughter tells stories good sense of humor can make fun of herself calls herself "little-miss-know-it-all" and "miss-smarty-pants" was frightened by a bear likes people good person understanding wise likes Winn-Dixie

Amanda	Feelings/Reactions
snob advanced reader brags walks right past Opal without looking at her tries to get Winn-Dixie and Opal in trouble pinch-faced	It makes me sad when Opal talks about her mother. She has her mother on her mind a lot. Even when something fun or interesting is happening, she is thinking about her mother. Hooray for Miss Franny! I like her. She knows what Amanda is doing and sticks up for Opal. Winn-Dixie makes me laugh. He's got such a great personality. People like Amanda are very annoying.

CHARACTER MAPS

Character maps are used to help students identify the traits of characters in a book as well as relationships between characters. After the students have read part of the book, the teacher or the students select at least two characters for analysis. Each character's name is placed near the top of a circle or box, and students list character traits under each of the names.

Next, the students draw an arrow from one character to another. Above and below the arrow, the students write words or phrases that tell how the first character feels about the second (e.g., "admires"), or what his or her relationship is to the second (e.g., "parent"). Several descriptors may be generated. A second arrow is drawn between these two characters, pointing in the opposite direction. Near this arrow the students write the second character's feelings about or relationship to the first.

Example 3.9

- **Title:** *Charlotte's Web*
- **Author:** E. B. White
- **Grade Level:** 3–6
- **Summary:** Charlotte is a clever spider who befriends a pig named Wilbur and, with the help of other animals, saves him from a sure death.

Character Map
(during Chapter 4)

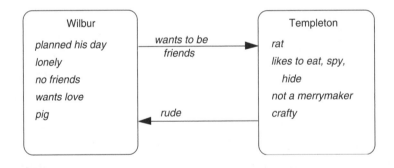

Character maps are useful in tracing the development of relationships. In the following example, two character maps are shown. The first was created by a class after reading the beginning the story. The second was written as students finished reading the story. These maps allow students to analyze the changes in characters as well as the changing relationships between characters.

Example 3.10

- **Title:** *Mike Mulligan and His Steam Shovel*
- **Author:** Virginia L. Burton
- **Grade Level:** K-2

■ **Summary:** Mike Mulligan is sad because he and his steam shovel, Mary Anne, have been replaced by new, modern equipment. In order to find work, he goes to a neighboring town where he meets Henry B. Swap, who intends to trick him into doing work for no pay. The story ends happily when Henry B. Swap appreciates Mike Mulligan's skills and stories.

Character Map
(Story Beginning)

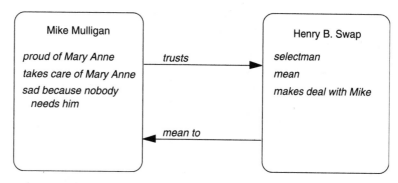

Character Map
(Story Ending)

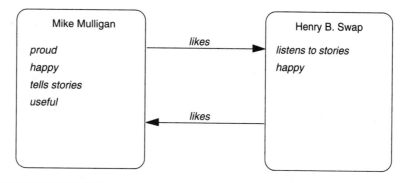

For more complex pieces of literature, several character maps might be developed. For example, in the book *Dragon's Gate*, by Laurence Yep, the young boy Otter greatly admires his Uncle Foxfire at the beginning of the book; is angry, bitter and disappointed with him later in the book; and then comes to understand and appreciate his uncle's courage and wisdom by the end of the book. The following three character maps illustrate changes that occur in the boy's perceptions of his uncle.

Example 3.11

■ **Title:** *Dragon's Gate*
■ **Author:** Laurence Yep
■ **Grade Level:** 5 and up

- **Summary:** Otter, a young Chinese boy, flees his country to join his legendary Uncle Foxfire and his father in America as they acquire new skills and knowledge by working on the transcontinental railroad. They plan to use this knowledge when they return to China to conduct the "Great Work." Otter is surprised by the working conditions and prejudice he encounters.

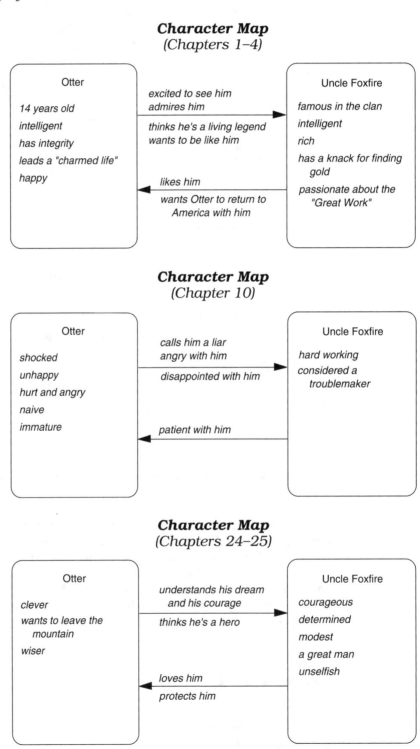

Character Map
(Chapters 1–4)

Otter		Uncle Foxfire
14 years old	excited to see him / admires him →	famous in the clan
intelligent	thinks he's a living legend / wants to be like him	intelligent
has integrity		rich
leads a "charmed life"	← likes him	has a knack for finding gold
happy	wants Otter to return to America with him	passionate about the "Great Work"

Character Map
(Chapter 10)

Otter		Uncle Foxfire
shocked	calls him a liar / angry with him →	hard working
unhappy	disappointed with him	considered a troublemaker
hurt and angry		
naive	← patient with him	
immature		

Character Map
(Chapters 24–25)

Otter		Uncle Foxfire
clever	understands his dream and his courage →	courageous
wants to leave the mountain	thinks he's a hero	determined
wiser		modest
	← loves him	a great man
	protects him	unselfish

CHARACTER WEBS

Another strategy for analyzing characters and facilitating discussions about them is character webbing. In this strategy, students identify character traits and cite examples from the text as evidence. Bromley (1996) has noted that webbing enhances comprehension and learning, links reading and writing, and promotes enjoyment. Character webbing draw readers back to the text as they look for supporting examples, and so their interactions with the text are enriched.

Webs are very flexible instructional tools, and there are a great variety of web types. The examples included here have at the center the name of a character. Circles placed around the center circle contain character traits. Branching off from these circles are supporting facts or information drawn from the text. For example, in the book *Doctor DeSoto,* by William Steig, students might decide that the doctor is clever, nice, cautious, and a good worker. After recording these traits in the circles, the students support their decisions by citing incidents from the story.

Example 3.12 _____

- **Title:** *Doctor DeSoto*
- **Author:** William Steig
- **Grade Level:** K-2
- **Summary:** A mouse dentist and his wife typically refuse to take dangerous animals as patients. However, when they are approached by a suffering fox, they make an exception. They discover that they had better protect themselves from being eaten, and they devise a clever plan to outsmart the fox.

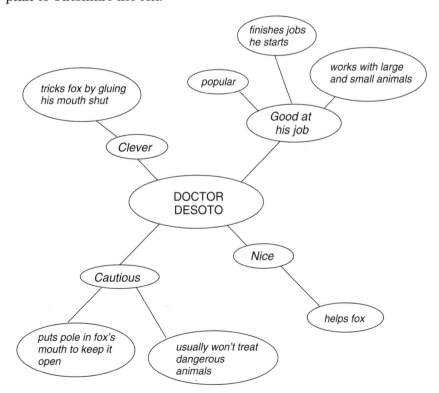

Example 3.13

- **Title:** *Crazy Lady!*
- **Author:** Jane Leslie Conly
- **Grade Level:** 6 and up
- **Summary:** A boy whose life has changed after the death of his mother slowly befriends the local alcoholic and her retarded son.

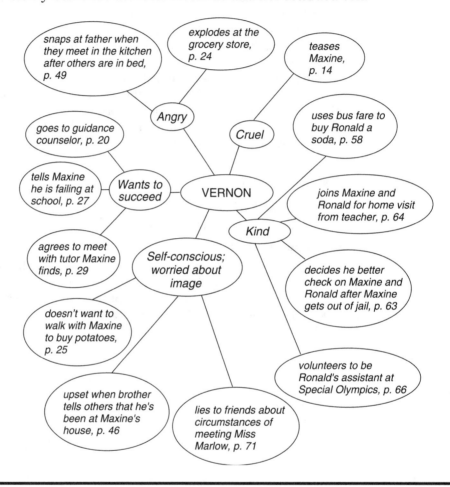

Example 3.14

- **Title:** *A Single Shard*
- **Author:** Linda Sue Park
- **Grade Level:** 4–8
- **Summary:** The young orphan Tree-ear lives under a bridge with Crane-man in twelfth-century Korea. Tree-ear longs to become a skilled potter. While admiring a piece made by the talented potter Min, Tree-ear accidentally breaks it. As payment, he works for the unfriendly Min. After proving himself worthy through hard work and loyalty, facing terrible danger on a journey to Songdo to show Min's pottery to the King's emissary, and losing his friend Crane-man, Tree-ear is finally welcomed by Min and granted the opportunity to learn to throw pots.

Character Web

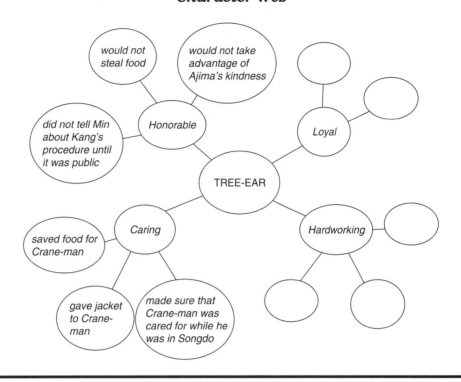

GRAPHIC ORGANIZERS

Graphic organizers are visual displays of relationships among ideas in a reading selection. They are used to help students organize information and to learn text structures. Graphic organizers support all students, and English learners in particular, by providing nonlinguistic representations of information in the text.

One type of graphic organizer is the story map. Most narrative text follows what is known as *story grammar*, or a set of rules by which a story is structured. Stories have characters and occur in a particular setting. The main character has a goal or confronts a problem, engages in a number of activities to achieve the goal or overcome the problem, and, ultimately, attains a resolution. Strategies that make story grammar explicit, such as story mapping in which students identify and record elements of narrative text, help students create and remember stories and support comprehension development (Baumann & Bergeron, 1993; Dickson, Simmons, & Kameenui, 1998; Dole, Brown, & Trathen, 1996; Leslie & Allan, 1999). Improved reading comprehension is more marked for less able readers (National Reading Panel, 2000).

Example 3.15 displays three maps for *Geraldine's Baby Brother*, by Holly Keller. First is a simple story map that helps students identify the beginning, middle, and end of stories. This is followed by more complex story maps that depict additional story elements.

Example 3.15 _____

- **Title:** *Geraldine's Baby Brother*
- **Author:** Holly Keller
- **Grade Level:** 1–3
- **Summary:** Geraldine is not happy that she has a new baby brother. She pouts and refuses to eat. The baby fusses and cries, and when Geraldine finds that she is the only one who can stop his crying, she decides he is not so bad after all.

Story Map 1

```
                    ┌────────────────────┐
                    │ GERALDINE'S BABY   │
                    │ BROTHER            │
                    └────────────────────┘
```

Beginning	Middle	End
Geraldine is not happy with her new baby brother and ignores him and others who try to be nice to her.	*The baby cries a lot and different family members try to get him to stop. Geraldine is not very nice to people.*	*Geraldine gets up in the night to tell the baby to stop crying and makes faces at him. He laughs, she reads to him and decides she likes him after all.*

Story Map 2

Basic Situation	Complications or Events	Resolution
Setting: *Geraldine's house* *Characters:* *Geraldine* *baby brother* *mother* *father* *aunt and uncle* *Mrs. Wilson* *Problem:* *Geraldine doesn't like her brother.*	*Geraldine puts on earmuffs so she can't hear the baby.* *Mrs. Wilson brings gifts for Geraldine and the baby. Geraldine doesn't open the gift.* *The baby cries a lot.* *No one can get the baby to stop crying.* *Her parents forget to feed her lunch.* *She goes to bed without dinner.*	*Geraldine gets up in the middle of the night to tell the baby to stop crying. She makes faces at him. He laughs and gurgles. She holds him and stays that way until morning.*

Story Map 3

Setting:

Characters:

Problem:

Event 1:

Event 2:

Event 3:

Solution:

Graphic organizers also support understanding of informational text. Informational texts often utilize one or more of the following organizational structures: description, sequence of events, cause-effect, problem-solution, and compare-contrast. Graphic organizers make these structures explicit to students, and students can use graphic organizers during reading to identify ideas in the texts as well as the relationships among them. Graphic organizers for the description text structure and sequence-of-events text structure are shared in Examples 3.16 and 3.17. Venn diagrams are useful for compare-contrast text structures and are shared in Chapter Four.

All of these graphic organizers are useful before, during, and after reading. We include them here because they provide a means for students to organize information as they read and reread a text. When they are used before reading, they provide a preview of text structure. When they are used after reading, they provide a scaffold for students' summaries of and reflections on text.

Example 3.16 _____

- **Title:** *Wonderful Worms*
- **Author:** Linda Glaser
- **Grade:** K–2
- **Summary:** The author shares interesting information about worms.

Graphic Organizer for Description Text Pattern

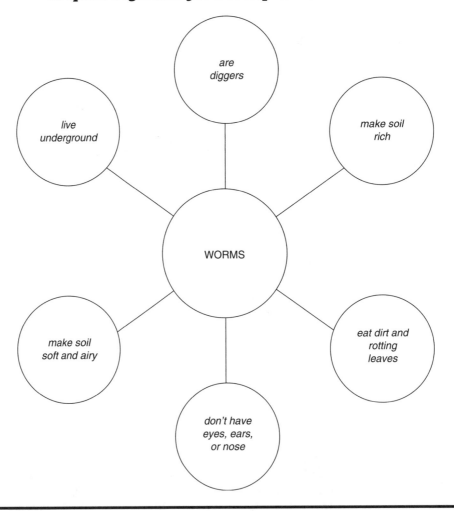

Example 3.17 _____

- **Title:** *Waiting for Wings*
- **Author:** Lois Ehlert
- **Grade:** K–3
- **Summary:** This beautifully illustrated book shares the life cycle of butterflies.

Graphic Organizer for Sequence of Events

Eggs cling to leaves.	Caterpillars hatch. They crawl and eat.	They make a case.

Inside the cases, they begin to change. They are becoming butterflies.	They break out of their cases and unfold their wings.	They fly to a garden to eat nectar from flowers.

CHARACTER PERSPECTIVE CHARTS

Although story mapping has been demonstrated to enhance students' understanding of narrative text, Shanahan and Shanahan (1997) have noted that story mapping can foster a misconception that there is only one possible interpretation of a story. Character perspective charts maintain the benefits of story mapping while at the same time promoting multiple interpretations. Instead of focusing on a single character and his or her problems, in character perspective charting, the students are guided to consider the story from more than one viewpoint (Shanahan & Shanahan, 1997).

Two examples of character perspective charts are displayed in Examples 3.18 and 3.19. In these examples, the teacher prepared a two-column chart that outlines the elements of story grammar in each column. In one column, the students responded to the prompts from one character's perspective, and in the other column, they responded to the prompts from a second character's perspective. Small groups of children who read the same book engaged in conversation and completed the chart together.

Example 3.18 _____

- **Title:** *Bread and Jam for Frances*
- **Author:** Russell Hoban
- **Grade Level:** 1–3
- **Summary:** Little Frances is interested in eating only her favorite food—bread and jam. She refuses to eat other foods that Mother prepares. She even trades away the lunch Mother packs for bread and jam sandwiches that her classmates have. Mother decides to let Frances eat only bread and jam for a while, and Frances discovers that eating only one type of food, even if it is a favorite, is not as desirable as it seems.

Character Perspective Chart

Main character: Who is the main character?	**Main character: Who is the main character?**
Frances	*Mother*
Setting: Where and when does the story take place?	**Setting: Where and when does the story take place?**
at home and at school	*at home*
Problem: What is the main character's problem?	**Problem: What is the main character's problem?**
Her mother is serving foods other than her favorite bread and jam.	*Her daughter won't try new foods.*
Goal: What is the main character's goal? What does the character want?	**Goal: What is the main character's goal? What does the character want?**
She wants to eat only bread and jam.	*She wants her daughter to try new foods and eat a variety of foods.*
Attempt: What does the main character do to solve the problem or get the goal?	**Attempt: What does the main character do to solve the problem or get the goal?**
She trades her food for bread and jam.	*She serves other foods at first, then she only serves bread and jam to Frances.*
Outcome: What happens as a result of the attempt?	**Outcome: What happens as a result of the attempt?**
Frances becomes tired of eating only bread and jam and eagerly eats other foods.	*Frances tries other foods.*
Reaction: How does the main character feel about the outcome?	**Reaction: How does the main character feel about the outcome?**
happy	*satisfied*
Theme: What point did the author want to make?	**Theme: What point did the author want to make?**
Try new things.	*The best strategy may be to let people discover some things for themselves.*

Example 3.19

- **Title:** *Walk Two Moons*
- **Author:** Sharon Creech
- **Grade Level:** 5–8
- **Summary:** In this award-winning novel, thirteen-year-old Salamanca travels across the country with her grandparents to the site where her

mother, having left home to find herself, was killed in a bus accident. Salamanca struggles with the fact that her mother left and will never return. While on the road trip, she tells her grandparents the story of her neighbor, Phoebe, whose mother also disappeared.

Character Perspective Chart

Main character: Who is the main character?	**Main character: Who is the main character?**
Salamanca Hiddle	*Phoebe Winterbottom*
Setting: Where and when does the story take place?	**Setting: Where and when does the story take place?**
on the road across the United States in the present	*in Euclid, Ohio, in the present*
Problem: What is the main character's problem?	**Problem: What is the main character's problem?**
Her mother left the family and is not returning.	*There has been a strange boy looking for Mrs. Winterbottom; Mrs. Winterbottom is behaving oddly; Mrs. Winterbottom leaves the family.*
Goal: What is the main character's goal? What does the character want?	**Goal: What is the main character's goal? What does the character want?**
She wants to reach her mother by her mother's birthday.	*She wants her mother to come home. She wants to find out who the boy is.*
Attempt: What does the main character do to solve the problem or get the goal?	**Attempt: What does the main character do to solve the problem or get the goal?**
She goes on a car trip with her grandparents, following her mother's route.	*She tries to convince others that the boy is a lunatic who has kidnapped her mother. She goes to the police. She tracks down the boy.*
Outcome: What happens as a result of the attempt?	**Outcome: What happens as a result of the attempt?**
She gets to Lewiston, her mother's final destination, by her mother's birthday.	*No one believes her. Her mother soon returns with the boy and everyone learns that the boy is her son.*
Reaction: How does the main character feel about the outcome?	**Reaction: How does the main character feel about the outcome?**
She accepts her mother's death and understands that her mother's decision to leave did not mean that her mother did not love her—the leaving was something separate from her love.	*She is both happy and angry.*

Theme: What point did the author want to make?	**Theme: What point did the the author want to make?**
Don't judge a man until you've walked two moons in his moccasins.	*Don't judge a man until you've walked two moons in his moccasins.*

In a similar activity that combines story mapping with consideration of multiple perspectives, Emery (1996) has recommended a three-column chart. In the middle column, students record the story problem, a list of important events that occur in the story, and the resolution. A different character's name is put at the top of each of the two remaining columns. Students engage in a discussion about the characters' perspectives on each of the elements listed in the middle column. Their ideas are recorded in the appropriate column immediately across from each of the story elements.

JOURNALS

Journal writing in response to a reading selection helps to move both younger and older students beyond literal comprehension to a more complete understanding of the content of a book (Barone, 1989) and encourages personal, thoughtful engagement with books (Fuhler, 1994). There are many types of journals. Double-entry journals, reading logs, partner journals, and character journals are described here.

The purpose of a double-entry journal is to allow students to select passages they find meaningful in a reading selection and then to write about why those passages are meaningful. Students may use 8½-by-11-inch lined paper that has been folded in half lengthwise. In the left-hand column, the student summarizes interesting information or copies verbatim a sentence or paragraph of his of her own choosing from the reading selection and records the page number. Directly across from the text information or quote, in the right-hand column, the student reacts to the passage. Selections and responses will vary widely. Some passages may be selected because they are funny or use interesting language. Others may be selected because they touch the student's heart or remind the student of experiences in his or her own life.

This activity encourages interaction between the selection and the students and gives each student a chance to identify what is meaningful to him or her. Students may choose to share their responses with one another or to keep them private. The double-entry journal may be used effectively with children as young as first-graders (Barone, 1990).

Example 3.20 _____

- **Title:** *Zzz . . . The Most Interesting Book You'll Ever Read about Sleep*
- **Author:** Trudee Romanek
- **Grade Level:** 2–6
- **Summary:** This book shares fascinating information about sleep, including stages of sleep, circadian rhythms, the consequences of lack of sleep, what scientists say about dreaming and sleepwalking, and more.

Double-Entry Journal

Quote	**Response**
Tests show that when a person stays up until 3 A.M., the next day their body has 30 percent fewer "natural killer cells"—the cells that fight viruses.	*My parents have told me that I need sleep in order to fight illness. Now I believe them!*
During Stage 4 [deep sleep], your body produces the largest amount of some of the chemicals that help you grow.	*This is really interesting and important. If I want to grow taller, I need to be sure to get plenty of sleep.*

Example 3.21

- **Title:** *Locomotion*
- **Author:** Jacqueline Woodson
- **Grade Level:** 5–8
- **Summary:** Lonnie Collins Motion's life changes when his parents die in a fire and he and his sister are sent to separate foster homes. A teacher helps him express his feelings, memories, and hopes in free verse. As Lonnie notes in the beginning, the entire book is a poem because every time he tries to tell the whole story, his mind goes Be Quiet!

Double-Entry Journal

Quote	**Response**
"Look at Little Brother Lonnie all growed up." (page 82)	*Rodney's saying this makes me happy and warm because it shows that Lonnie was accepted by Rodney as a part of the family. What a great, great guy Rodney is. Lonnie's reaction made me feel even better, almost as if I were him. I was so happy I almost cried.*
"You think it's still flying through the air somewhere?" (page 86)	*Wow. This is a really different thought. I can picture a kiss you blow flying through the air. How sad that Lonnie wonders if his kiss ever made it to his parents the night they died. He wonders if it's just floating out there somewhere. I can't imagine having your parents die without warning and never getting to say good-bye. I'll never think of blown kisses in the same way.*

Reading logs, or literature logs, are more directed than double-entry journals in that the teacher provides a prompt for writing following a period of sustained silent reading or a shared reading experience. Kelly and Farnan (1991) have argued that reading logs can be effective in promoting the critical thinking skills of analysis and evaluation and in promoting personal interactions with text if the appropriate prompts are provided. Appropriate prompts are those that elicit a reader's perception of, association with, or evaluation of the text. Kelly and Farnan have provided a list of sixteen "reader-response" prompts, including the following: "What character was your favorite? Why?" "What character did you dislike? Why?" "Are you like any character in the story? Explain." "Does anything in this work remind you of your own life or something that happened to you?" "What was your first reaction to the story?" "If you were a teacher, would you read this book to your class?"

Each of these questions emphasizes the students' personal interpretations and interactions with the text. Non–reader-response prompts are those that focus exclusively on the text, such as "Tell me about your book." When the reader-response prompts were used with fourth-grade students, Kelly and Farnan found that students went beyond a literal response to the text and engaged in thinking that involved analysis of text from a variety of perspectives.

Example 3.22

- **Title:** *Flip-Flop Girl*
- **Author:** Katherine Paterson
- **Grade Level:** 4–6
- **Summary:** When Vinnie's father dies, her brother stops speaking, and her mother can't make ends meet, the family moves across the county to live with Vinnie's grandmother. This book tells the story of the pain a young girl experiences when everything in her life seems to go wrong, and the special friendship that develops with a classmate who saves her brother.

Reading Log

Prompt (after reading Chapter Two): Does anything in this chapter remind you of something that has happened to you?

Response:

I guess I'm really lucky. I have been going to this school since kindergarten. I can just imagine how awful it would be to leave your friends and move to a new place. I wouldn't want to be brand-new in a school where everybody else already knows each other. Vinnie must feel terrible, especially with everything else that's going on in her life. And Heather was mean. I'm glad that the teacher seems so nice.

Partner journals (sometimes referred to as dialogue journals) require students to interact with another person, often a peer. The students may react to a chapter after it is read or the teacher may offer prompts. Once the writing is completed, students exchange journals with a partner who responds to their comments. This exchange may occur immediately or after a day or two have elapsed. Partners may be anonymous, each student having a secret identification number or name, or may be known. If two classes are reading the same book, journals may be exchanged across classes. Partner journals stimulate purposeful communication, provide an opportunity for writing, and allow for feedback from peers (Bromley, 1989). Morgan and Albritton (1990) have reported success with this activity with children as young as second-graders and found that both the content and the form of student writing improved over time.

Example 3.23

- ■ **Title:** *A Gathering of Days*
- ■ **Author:** Joan Blos
- ■ **Grade Level:** 4–6
- ■ **Summary:** Written in journal format, this book tells the story of two years in the life of a nineteenth-century New England girl.

Partner Journal

Dear Journal Partner:

This book is so cool! I have a diary, but I'm not very good about writing in it. Do you suppose someone will want to publish it someday?! Who do you think "the phantom" is that she has seen twice now?

Your Partner

Dear Partner:

I don't know who the phantom is. The book tells about bound boys who should be returned when they run away. Do you suppose the phantom is a boy who ran away? I wonder if Aunt Lucy is going to end up marrying the father.

I don't have a diary, but I think it would be fun to write in one. You could tell secrets to your diary that you wouldn't dare tell anyone else!

Your Partner

Family members can be included in the journal experience also. If the family member has read the book, both he or she and the student can respond to the literature, sharing their points of view and their reactions. If the family member has not read the book, then he or she can respond to the student's comments by asking questions, requesting clarification, and reacting to the student's comments. In example 3.24, a second-grade child read *Sea Turtles* in class, wrote in his partner journal, then took the book and the journal home to his parents. Both parents responded. The book and journal were returned to school several days later. The boy waited until he was at school to read his parents' responses.

Fuhler (1994) described an experience she had with her junior high students and their parents in which the parents were invited to read the same book as their children and to participate in a dialogue about the book through the use of a partner journal. She found that most parents were delighted to be involved in the activity, and she was impressed with the thoughtful responses made by both parents and students.

Example 3.24 _____

- **Title:** *Sea Turtles*
- **Author:** Gail Gibbons
- **Grade Level:** K–2
- **Summary:** The author describes the variety of sea turtles, discusses their habits, explains people's efforts to protect them, and compares them to land turtles. This book is rich in information and a useful resource for young readers.

Partner Journal

Dear Mom and Dad:

I like reading about sea turtles. They are my favorite animal. Did you know they live a long, long time? Can I see one sometime?

Dan

Dear Dan:

This was an interesting book! It is fascinating that sea turtles can live to be over 100 years old! I learned other things about sea turtles that I never knew. For instance, I didn't know that sea turtles have been around for millions of years. Wow! I also didn't know that they lay about 100 eggs at a time! Imagine a human mother having 100 babies!!

I hope we will see a sea turtle some time. Maybe we can go to the aquarium soon.

Love,

Dad

Hi Danny!

I had desert tortoises when I was young. They used to hibernate in the winter. We never knew quite where they went—one day we'd go outside and couldn't find them. Then, months later, they'd reappear! I learned from your book that sea turtles disappear too! They don't hibernate, but they do migrate—travel a long distance away—when they are going to have their young.

Share another book with me soon!

Love,

Mom

In character journals, suggested by Hancock (1993) and Van Horn (1997), students assume the voice of a character as they record their feelings about story events. Hancock has stated that when students are encouraged "to step inside [a character's] mind and heart and compose a personal response from his [or her] point of view" (p. 42), a high level of involvement and identification is attained. Readers grow in their understanding of the actions, motives, and emotions of the character. Hancock found in working with her eighth-grade students that they also needed the opportunity to react from their own perspectives, however. Students' personal entries can be set off in parentheses to distinguish them from the voice of the main character. By thinking about story events from both the character's perspective and their own perspectives, students may gain insights into their own values and ideals, thus gaining a greater sense of their identities—adding a powerful dimension to this type of journal.

Example 3.25 _____

- **Title:** *Surviving the Applewhites*
- **Author:** Stephanie S. Tolan
- **Grade Level:** 4–6
- **Summary:** After being expelled from middle school, Jake Semple is home-schooled by the Applewhites, a family of interesting personalities with many and diverse talents. Through his relationships with the family and his involvement in their adventurous quests for the meaning of life, Jake finds himself and learns what brings him joy. At the same time, twelve-year-old E. D. Applewhite and her family come to appreciate her special talent for organization.

Character Journal

Dear Journal,

Yesterday I met Jake. He's disgusting. He smokes and swears and has scarlet spiked hair, an eyebrow ring, and earrings. Yes, earrings. Lots of them. I can't believe my family wants me to work with him on my curriculum plan. The whole point of the Applewhite Creative Academy is to follow your own interests and create your own plan for learning. Everybody works alone on what interests them. I don't want to have to share my plan with Jake, but everybody says I have to because we are in the same place in math, because Jake needs structure, and because Jake needs cooperative learning. They say I'm the only cooperative one in the family. I guess it doesn't pay to be cooperative.

Until tomorrow,

E. D.

When teachers respond to journals, it is important that they focus on the message and not the form of the students' writing. Teachers should limit correction of spelling, punctuation, and syntax (although they should use their observations of students' developing writing skills to inform instruction) while modeling standard usage as they respond in writing to the content of students' entries. Responses should be nonjudgmental, encouraging, and thought stretching (Fuhler, 1994; Hancock, 1993). An emphasis on students' ideas is particularly supportive of English learners because real and purposeful dialogue is promoted, a nonthreatening context for writing is established because the work is not "corrected," and teacher responses provide a model of effective writing and elaboration.

Journals provide readers with the opportunity to think about and share their feelings and thoughts about characters, events, and ideas throughout their reading of a book. They give students a voice in their reading, and allow them to collaborate with an author as they create meaning together (Fuhler, 1994). A variety of journal formats should be used throughout the course of a school year, because each type provides a different kind of experience for both the teacher and the student. Double-entry journals, reading logs, partner journals, and character journals are just four of many journal formats. Edwards (1991–92) has described several other exciting formats that she has found useful in promoting critical thinking skills.

FEELINGS CHARTS

A feelings chart is useful in helping students analyze characters' reactions to one or more events in a piece of literature. The chart also may serve as a vehicle for comparing and contrasting characters and is beneficial in building vocabulary.

The teacher prepares by identifying several events that occur in the reading selection and then listing the characters who are influenced by the event. Events are listed, as in Example 3.26, down the side of a chart. Characters are listed across the top of the chart. As the students read or listen to a selection, they are asked to provide a one-word description of each character's feelings at the time of each event. Their descriptions are written where the respective characters and the events intersect on the chart.

Example 3.26 _____

- **Title:** *The Wave*
- **Author:** Margaret Hodges
- **Grade Level:** 2–3
- **Summary:** The people of a village in Japan are threatened by a destructive tidal wave. Only an old man who resides at the top of a hill sees the danger. He attempts to warn the villagers by burning his precious rice fields.

Feelings Chart

Events	Characters		
	Ojiisan	Tada	Villagers
The water was calm and the village children played in the gentle waves.	*content* *satisfied* *happy*	*glad* *happy* *playful*	*thankful* *secure* *lucky* *peaceful* *cheerful*

Events	Characters		
	Ojiisan	Tada	Villagers
Ojiisan sets fire to the rice fields.	*awful* *bad* *sad* *worried*	*anxious* *puzzled* *curious* *upset* *horrified*	*excited* *surprised* *unlucky* *vengeful* *angry* *crazy*
The huge tidal wave strikes the beach.	*afraid* *hopeful* *thankful*	*scared* *afraid* *panic*	*scared* *frightened* *terrified* *afraid*
The villagers, Ojisan, and Tada look down upon the empty beach where their village used to stand.	*successful* *relieved* *right*	*proud* *amazed*	*lucky* *thankful* *sad* *dazed* *forgiving* *grateful* *horrified* *amazed* *shocked*

Students may develop charts in small groups or the teacher may facilitate the development of a whole-class chart.

Three student teachers modeled an interesting approach to this activity in a university seminar. The student teachers displayed the chart

identifying key events in the story in the front of the room and then read the book aloud, pausing after each event. At each pause, they distributed small self-adhesive pieces of paper to everyone in the class and directed those students sitting on the right side of the classroom to write a single word that described how Ojiisan felt at the time. Students in the center of the classroom each wrote a word describing how Tada felt, and those students on the left side of the classroom wrote a word describing the feelings of the villagers. Each member of the class was permitted to write only one word. Then students, one row at a time, were instructed to bring their paper to the chart and post it on the chart in the appropriate place. After all papers had been displayed, each contribution was read and discussed. The variety of words generated by the class was astounding, and the reaction from the students was one of interest and curiosity. The responses in Example 3.26 are a sampling of those given by the university students. Some students may wish to include a column labeled "Me" so they have an opportunity to respond to the events as well.

Example 3.27 _____

- **Poem:** "Casey at the Bat"
- **Book:** *The Family Book of Best Loved Poems* (David L. George, ed.)
- **Poet:** Ernest Lawrence Thayer
- **Grade Level:** 5 and up
- **Summary:** Fans count on Casey to win the baseball game. When he strikes out, it is a sad day in the history of Mudville.

Feelings Chart

Events	Characters		
	Casey	The Crowd	Me
Casey steps up to bat.			
The umpire calls, "Strike Two!"			
Casey strikes out.			

CONTRAST CHARTS

Contrast charts are described in Chapter Two as a prereading activity. These charts are also useful during reading as a means for recording contrasting ideas or information in a selection as it is read. For example, students may list the pros and cons of an issue, the advantages and disadvantages of a course of action, or the two sides of an argument as they are described in the selection. Once information from the selection has been organized in this manner, the chart may serve as a guide for writing. In Example 3.28, students record a character's reasons for and against taking a teddy bear to a sleepover while they are reading or listening to the story.

Example 3.28 _____

- **Title:** *Ira Sleeps Over*
- **Author:** Bernard Waber
- **Grade Level:** K-3
- **Summary:** Ira has been invited to spend the night at a friend's house. He is very excited until his sister asks him whether he plans to take along his teddy bear. Ira wrestles with this question because he doesn't want to appear babyish to his friend, but he has never slept without "TaTa."

Contrast Chart

Reasons Why Ira Should Take His Teddy Bear	Reasons Why Ira Should Not Take His Teddy Bear
He's never slept without it.	*His friend will laugh at him.*
They're going to tell scary stories.	*He'll think Ira is a baby.*
His friend's house is very dark.	*His friend will laugh at the bear's name.*

Example 3.29 _____

- **Title:** *Running Out of Time*
- **Author:** Margaret Peterson Haddix
- **Grade Level:** 4–6
- **Summary:** When Jessie's mother asks her to leave their village to seek medical assistance for those suffering from an outbreak of diphtheria, Jessie discovers that the year is not 1840 as she has been led to believe. Instead, the year is 1996 and she is part of an experiment by unethical scientists and her community is a tourist attraction that is observed by modern-day people. Jessie faces a very different world when she escapes her village.

Contrast Chart

Life in the 1840s	Life in the 1990s
1.	1.
2.	2.
3.	3.
4.	4.
5.	5.
6.	6.
7.	7.
8.	8.
9.	9.
10.	10.

Example 3.30 _____

- **Title:** *The Call of the Wild*
- **Author:** Jack London
- **Grade Level:** 7 and above
- **Summary:** Buck is a well-cared-for family dog who is taken from his comfortable home in the south to serve as sled dog in the Alaskan wilderness.

Contrast Chart

Life in the South	Life in the North
1.	1.
2.	2.
3.	3.
4.	4.
5.	5.

TEN IMPORTANT WORDS

The ten important words activity supports students' active engagement with text as they read to identify important words in a selection, compare their words to those selected by peers, and then write a one-sentence summary of the selection (Yopp & Yopp, 2003). First, each student is provided with a copy of a reading selection and a set of self-adhesive notes. The teacher instructs the students to independently identify the ten most important words in the text as they read—that is, the words that capture the most significant ideas in the selection—and record one word on each of ten self-adhesive notes. As the students silently read the selection, they choose and record words, revise their choices with continued reading, choose additional words, reread the selection, and make final decisions about word choices.

When each of the students has settled on a personal set of ten words, the teacher assists the students in building a group bar graph of the words and then leads a discussion about this visual display of the students' word choices. What patterns are seen? Which words were frequently selected by students? Why were some words selected by so many students? Which words are unique? Why might those words have been chosen by a member of the class? What does a particular word mean? Observations about the word selections stimulate discussion about the content of the text, and students elaborate on their word choices by explaining how the word is used in the text. After selecting ten important words from Gail Gibbons's *From Seed to Plant,* one student might volunteer, "I chose *wind* because the wind blows pollen from flower to flower, and this is what seeds need to grow." Another might say, "I chose *travel* because seeds sometimes travel far from the plant they grew on because they're carried away by birds or water or wind." Students are usually quite interested in the choices of their peers and often comment on why they did or did not choose the same word as others in the class, what they found most interesting in the text,

and how they might reconsider their choices now that they have talked with their peers about the words and the reading selection.

After the discussion, each student writes a one-sentence summary of the text. Their own reading of the text, their selection of important words, and their discussion with peers support the students' efforts to summarize the text. Summaries usually reflect a deep understanding of the reading selection that results from the thoughtful interactions with the text and peers about the important ideas. Example 3.31 shares one student's ten important words and summary.

The emphasis on vocabulary and big ideas in the reading selection, the oral elaboration of ideas in the text as students discuss word choices, and the visual display of word selections support English learners in their efforts to negotiate meaning in the text and to use academic language to summarize the text. Further, because student names are not written on the self-adhesive notes, participation is low risk and students feel comfortable contributing to the chart. Additional support can be provided by allowing students to select their ten important words with a partner in the first step of this activity if the material is challenging.

Example 3.31

- **Title:** *Spinning Spiders*
- **Author:** Melvin Berger
- **Grade Level:** K–3
- **Summary:** Many interesting facts about the variety of spider webs, the manner in which they are spun, and the purposes they serve are shared in this book.

Ten Important Words

spiders

spiderwebs

arachnids

spinnerets

different

threads

silk

sticky

prey

insects

Summary Sentence: *Thousands of types of eight-legged arachnids use their spinnerets to make strong, sticky, silk thread that they weave into different kinds of webs to capture and wrap up their insect prey.*

In Example 3.32, students worked in pairs to select words, built a class graph, and then wrote summary statements with their partner. They did this at two points during their reading of *Harvesting Hope: The Story of Cesar Chavez*, by Kathleen Krull, first as they read about Chavez's early life in the beginning of the book and later as they read about his protest years. Working their way through the text in this manner, the students built brief summaries that captured key ideas from the book. The work of one pair of students is shared in this example, and it reveals that students may select short phrases that represent an idea (e.g., "La Causa" and "National Farm Workers Association").

Example 3.32 _____

- **Title:** *Harvesting Hope: The Story of Cesar Chavez*
- **Author:** Kathleen Krull
- **Grade Level:** K–6
- **Summary:** In this Pura Belpré Honor Book, readers learn about Cesar Chavez's early years and his peaceful protest against the conditions of California farm workers.

Ten Important Words
(first part of the book)

Chavez

ranch

drought

landowners

school

farms

California

migrants

fields

powerless

Summary Sentence: *Chavez's family had to leave their ranch in Arizona after a drought and go to California where they became migrant workers and lived and worked in terrible conditions.*

Ten Important Words
(second part of the book)

change

nonviolence

fight

La Causa

National Farm Workers Association

huelga

grapes

march

capitol

contract

Summary Sentence: *Chavez organized a huelga (strike) and a march to the state capitol to fight for change with talk, not violence.*

CONCLUSION

During-reading activities enhance students' understanding of a text by prompting the use of comprehension strategies; facilitating thinking about ideas, text elements, or language; and promoting collaborative constructions of meaning. They also prompt personal responses to literature. During-reading activities engage students with a text, inviting them to think deeply about what they are reading and to share their thinking with peers.

REFERENCES

Atwater, R., & Atwater, F. (1966). *Mr. Popper's penguins.* New York: Little, Brown.

Barone, D. (1989). Young children's written responses to literature: The relationship between written response and orthographic knowledge. In S. McCormick & J. Zutell (Eds.), *Cognitive and social perspectives for literacy research and instruction* (pp. 371–379). Chicago: National Reading Conference.

Barone, D. (1990). The written responses of young children: Beyond comprehension to story understanding. *The New Advocate, 3* (1), 49–56.

Baumann, J. F., & Bergeron, B. S. (1993). Story map instruction using children's literature: Effects on first graders' comprehension of central narrative elements. *Journal of Reading Behavior, 25,* 407–437.

Berger, M. (2003). *Spinning spiders.* New York: HarperCollins.

Blos, J. W. (1979). *A gathering of days.* New York: Macmillan.

Bromley, K. (1989). Buddy journals make the reading-writing connection. *The Reading Teacher, 43,* 122–129.

Bromley, K. (1996). *Webbing with literature: Creating story maps with children's books.* Boston: Allyn and Bacon.

Burton, V. L. (1967). *Mike Mulligan and his steam shovel.* Boston: Houghton Mifflin.

Cleary, B. (1975). *Ramona and her father.* New York: Dell.

Conly, J. L. (1993). *Crazy lady!* New York: HarperCollins.

Creech, S. (1996). *Walk two moons.* New York: HarperTrophy.

Daniels, H. (1994). *Literature circles: Voice and choice in the student-centered classroom.* York, ME: Stenhouse.

DiCamillo, K. (2000). *Because of Winn-Dixie.* Cambridge, MA: Candlewick.

Dickson, S. V., Simmons, D. C., & Kameenui, E. J. (1998). Text organization: Research bases. In D. C. Simmons & E. J. Kameenui (Eds.), *What reading research tells us about children with diverse learning needs: Bases and basics* (pp. 239–277). Mahwah, NJ: Erlbaum.

Dole, J. A., Brown, K. J., & Trathen, W. (1996). The effects of strategy instruction on the comprehension performance of at-risk students. *Reading Research Quarterly, 31,* 62–88.

Eastman, P. D. (1960). *Are you my mother?* New York: Beginner Books.

Edwards, P. (1991–92). Using dialectical journals to teach thinking skills. *Journal of Reading, 35,* 312–316.

Ehlert, L. (2001). *Waiting for wings.* San Diego: Harcourt.

Emery, D. (1996). Helping readers comprehend stories from the characters' perspectives. *The Reading Teacher, 49,* 534–541.

Fuhler, C. (1994). Response journals: Just one more time with feeling. *Journal of Reading, 37,* 400–405.

Gibbons, G. (1993). *From seed to plant.* New York: Holiday House.

Gibbons, G. (1995). *Sea turtles.* New York: Holiday House.

Glaser, L. (1992). *Wonderful worms.* Brookfield, CT: Millbrook.

Haddix, M. (1995). *Running out of time.* New York: Aladdin.

Hancock, M. (1993). Character journals: Initiating involvement and identification through literature. *Journal of Reading, 37,* 42–50.

Haskell, S. (1987). Literature mapping. *The California Reader, 20,* 29–31.

Henkes, K. (2003). *Olive's ocean.* New York: Greenwillow.

Hiaasen, C. (2002). *Hoot.* New York: Knopf.

Hoban, R. (1993). *Bread and jam for Frances.* New York: HarperCollins.

Hobbs, W. (1989). *Bearstone.* New York: Avon.

Hodges, M. (1964). *The wave.* Boston: Houghton Mifflin.

Keller, H. (1994). *Geraldine's baby brother.* New York: Morrow.

Kelly, P., & Farnan, N. (1991). Promoting critical thinking through response logs: A reader-response approach with fourth graders. In J. Zutell & S. McCormick (Eds.), *Learner factors/Teacher factors: Issues in literacy research and instruction.* Fortieth Yearbook of the National Reading Conference. Chicago: National Reading Conference.

Krull, K. (2003). *Harvesting hope: The story of Cesar Chavez.* San Diego, CA: Harcourt.

Leslie, L., & Allen, L. (1999). Factors that predict success in an early literacy intervention project. *Reading Research Quarterly, 34,* 404–424.

London, J. (1974). *Call of the wild.* New York: Simon & Schuster.

Morgan, R., & Albritton, J. D. (1990). Primary students respond to literature through partner journals. *The California Reader, 23,* 29–30.

National Reading Panel. (2000). *Teaching children to read: An evidence-based assessment of scientific research literature on reading and its implications for reading instruction* (NIH Publication No. 00–4769). Washington, DC: U.S. Government Printing Office.

O'Dell, S. (1960). *Island of the Blue Dolphins.* New York: Dell.

Park, L.S. (2001). *A single shard.* New York: Clarion.

Paterson, K. (1994). *Flip-flop girl.* New York: Lodestar.

Romanek, T. (2002). *Zzz . . . The most interesting book you'll ever read about sleep.* Toronto: Kids Can Press.

Shanahan, T., & Shanahan, S. (1997). Character perspective charting: Helping children to develop a more complete conception of story. *The Reading Teacher, 50,* 668–677.

Steig, W. (1982). *Doctor DeSoto.* New York: Farrar, Straus & Giroux.

Thayer, E. L. (1952). Casey at the bat. In David L. George (Ed.), *The family book of best loved poems* (pp. 411–412). Garden City, NY: Hanover House.

Tolan, S. (2002). *Surviving the Applewhites.* New York: HarperTrophy.

Van Horn, L. (1997). The characters within us: Readers connect with characters to create meaning and understanding. *Journal of Adolescent and Adult Literacy, 40,* 342–347.

Waber, B. (1975). *Ira sleeps over.* Boston: Houghton Mifflin.

White, E. B. (1952). *Charlotte's web.* New York: Harper & Row.

Woodson, J. (2003). *Locomotion.* New York: Grosset & Dunlap.

Yep, L. (1993). *Dragon's gate.* New York: HarperCollins.

Yopp, H. K., & Yopp, R. H. (2003). Ten important words: Identifying the big ideas in informational text. *Journal of Content Area Reading, 2,* 7–13.

CHAPTER FOUR

Postreading Activities

Postreading

Purposes

- To encourage personal responses
- To stimulate thinking
- To identify what is meaningful
- To promote reflection
- To facilitate organization, analysis, and synthesis
- To share and build interpretations
- To prompt connections

Activities

- Polar opposites
- Powerful passages
- Literary report cards
- Plot profiles
- Venn diagrams
- Book charts
- Poetic responses
- Sketch to stretch
- 3-D responses

The postreading activities students engage in will have an impact on how they view the reading selection as well as the reading act. If students reflect on important ideas, share reactions, return to the book to achieve greater understanding, make connections with what they have read, engage thoughtfully with peers, and creatively respond to the literature, the selection will be viewed as a source of enjoyment and will be long remembered. Reading will be viewed as a meaningful and satisfying activity. If, on the other hand, students answer a series of low-level questions, work quietly, prove that they can sequence events by numbering them on a worksheet, and complete a crossword puzzle to reinforce vocabulary, then they are likely to view the selection as simply a vehicle for skills instruction. Reading will be perceived as an exercise.

The postreading activities we provide in this chapter are in keeping with the reasons for using literature in the classroom. In particular, they promote enjoyment of reading by encouraging personal responses to literature, stimulating thinking about ideas and issues in books, and inviting students to identify what is meaningful to them. They deepen students' understandings of the book by providing structures to help students reflect on the text; organize, analyze, and synthesize information and ideas; and share and build interpretations with peers. They promote extension of comprehension beyond the text as students make connections among books and with their own lives.

The first activity, *polar opposites,* gives students a framework for thinking about characters. It requires analysis of characters' behaviors and the author's language in order to draw conclusion about traits. *Powerful passages* prompt students to revisit the literature to identify interesting or powerful ideas, events, and language to share with peers. *Literary report cards* provide a motivating format for thinking about and discussing characters. *Plot profiles* provide a graphic means for organizing and analyzing the plot of a story. *Venn diagrams* facilitate comparisons between two or more characters, events, or books, or between a character and the readers themselves. *Book charts* are useful for examining several books by the same author, on the same topic, or with the same theme. *Poetic responses, sketch to stretch,* and *3-D responses* invite students to capture the essence of a reading selection and creatively express it.

Thus, the postreading activities presented in this chapter may be used for the following purposes:

- To encourage personal responses
- To stimulate thinking about ideas and issues
- To invite students to identify what is meaningful to them
- To promote reflection on the text
- To facilitate organization, analysis, and synthesis of information and ideas
- To provide opportunities for sharing and building interpretations with peers
- To prompt connections among books and with students' lives

Students at all levels of reading development can participate meaningfully in the activities presented in this chapter. The activities promote higher-level thinking while also providing scaffolds for students' rich interactions with the literature. Several of the activities reduce linguistic demands by providing opportunities for nonlinguistic representations of understandings and responses. The activities invite diverse and creative responses that honor the reader.

POLAR OPPOSITES

The polar opposites activity provides a structure for students to analyze characters in a reading selection. Students rate characters on a variety of traits and draw examples from the text to support their ratings.

To develop a polar opposites guide, the teacher begins by selecting a character and generating a list of traits that describe him or her. Then the teacher identifies the opposite of each of those traits. For example, if a character is very sure of himself, has many friends, and is easily angered, the list might include "confident," "popular," and "hot-tempered." Opposites of these might be "unsure," "unpopular," and "easygoing." Opposites used will depend on the precise meaning intended by the initial term. Each pair of opposites makes up its own scale, as seen in the examples that follow. After reading a selection, students rate the character(s) by placing a mark on each scale.

Students may work individually to rate characters, or they may work in pairs or small groups and come to consensus. Alternatively, the teacher may provide a large chart in the classroom that displays several scales onto which students record their ratings with tally marks. In this way, student opinions are compiled in one place and students can see what the prevailing and minority opinions are at a glance.

In Example 4.1, we have placed an *X* on each scale to show possible student responses. Responses will vary.

Example 4.1

- **Poem:** "The Road Not Taken"
- **Book:** *You Come Too* (Robert Frost)
- **Poet:** Robert Frost
- **Grade Level:** 4 and up
- **Summary:** A traveler reflects on his decision to take a less traveled road.

Polar Opposites

The traveler was

thoughtful	_X_	____	____	____	____	impulsive
timid	____	____	____	_X_	____	courageous
disappointed	____	____	____	_X_	____	content
realistic	____	_X_	____	____	____	unrealistic
a follower	____	____	____	____	_X_	a leader

Nowhere in the poem does the poet explicitly state that the traveler is thoughtful or impulsive, timid or courageous, disappointed or content, and so on. Students must examine the traveler's behaviors and thoughts in order to form judgments.

Students then discuss their ratings with classmates. It is during discussion that students give voice to their ideas and their mental processes become public. Readers who may be having difficulty interpreting the text are exposed to the thinking of peers as reasons for ratings are shared and evidence from the text is cited. Further, students may be exposed to multiple perspectives and ways of thinking about the text. Any rating should be considered acceptable as long as students support their responses with information from the text or from their own knowledge or experiences.

When constructing the polar opposites, the teacher decides how many points to include on the scale based on his or her knowledge of the students. A three-point scale is used in Example 4.2. *The Story of Ferdinand*, by Munro Leaf, is generally read with young children who may have difficulty making the finer discriminations required on scales with more points. In this example, students write responses or dictate them to an adult prior to or as they engage in discussion.

Example 4.2

- **Title:** *The Story of Ferdinand*
- **Author:** Munro Leaf
- **Grade Level:** K–1
- **Summary:** Ferdinand the bull is very different from other bulls. He is big and strong, but he is not interested in butting heads and fighting. He prefers to sit and smell flowers.

Polar Opposites

Ferdinand is

happy   _X_   _____ _____ sad

He seems to be very happy as long as he can sit and smell flowers. He was even happy in the bull's ring because he could smell the flowers in the ladies' hair.

healthy   _X_   _____ _____ unhealthy

He is big and strong, which means he must be healthy.

fierce   _____ _____ _X_ tame

Ferdinand likes to sit. He is not interested in fighting.

same   _____ _____ _X_ different

Ferdinand is different from other bulls. He is happy sitting, and the others like to fight and butt heads. He was not interested in being picked for the bull's ring. Other bulls tried hard to be picked.

brave   _X_   _____ _____ fearful

He must be fairly brave because he did what he wanted to do even though it was not like other bulls. Also, he did not seem upset about going into the bull's ring.

Example 4.3

- **Title:** *Amazing Grace*
- **Author:** Mary Hoffman
- **Grade Level:** K–3
- **Summary:** Grace loves acting out stories. When her teacher announces that the class will present the play *Peter Pan*, Grace wants to play Peter. Friends tell her that she cannot be Peter Pan because she is a girl and she is black. Grace's mother and grandmother assure her that she can be anything she wants to be, and she impresses her classmates with a fantastic audition. She gets the part and the play is a success.

Polar Opposites

Grace is

happy	_____	_____	_____	_____	sad
timid	_____	_____	_____	_____	brave
imaginative	_____	_____	_____	_____	unimaginative
liked	_____	_____	_____	_____	disliked

Example 4.4

- **Title:** *The Watsons Go to Birmingham—1963*
- **Author:** Christopher Paul Curtis
- **Grade Level:** 5–8
- **Summary:** In this humorous and deeply moving book, a black family from Michigan travels to Alabama during the height of the civil rights movement. The family encounters violence, and Byron, the oldest sibling, helps his brother recover from the wrenching experience of the bombing of a neighborhood church.

Polar Opposites

Byron is

mean	_____	_____	_____	_____	_____	kind
insensitive	_____	_____	_____	_____	_____	sensitive
disrespectful	_____	_____	_____	_____	_____	respectful
not likable	_____	_____	_____	_____	_____	likable
unintelligent	_____	_____	_____	_____	_____	intelligent

Example 4.5

- **Title:** *A Corner of the Universe*
- **Author:** Ann M. Martin
- **Grade Level:** 4–6

- **Summary:** Eleven-year-old Hattie is surprised to learn she has an Uncle Adam when he moves in with her grandparents one summer. Adam is mentally ill and his behavior is sometimes frightening but Hattie loves and appreciates him, and he changes her life.

Polar Opposites

Hattie is

shy	_____	_____	_____	_____	outgoing
brave	_____	_____	_____	_____	timid
kind	_____	_____	_____	_____	unkind
obedient	_____	_____	_____	_____	disobedient
happy	_____	_____	_____	_____	unhappy
impulsive	_____	_____	_____	_____	thoughtful

A modification of the polar opposites activity is presented in Example 4.6. In *From the Mixed-Up Files of Mrs. Basil E. Frankweiler,* by E. L. Konigsburg, two characters have contrasting traits and may be rated on the same scales. Students write a "C" for Claudia and a "J" for Jamie at the appropriate point on each scale. Similarly, in Example 4.7, two characters from *Lily's Crossing,* by Patricia Reilly Giff, are rated on the same scales.

Example 4.6 _____

- **Title:** *From the Mixed-Up Files of Mrs. Basil E. Frankweiler*
- **Author:** E. L. Konigsburg
- **Grade Level:** 5–6
- **Summary:** Two children, Claudia and Jamie, run away from home and hide in a museum where they solve a mystery.

Polar Opposites

tightwad	_J_	_____	_____	_C_	big spender
cautious	_____	_C_	_J_	_____	adventurous
predictable	_____	_C_	_____	_J_	spontaneous
messy	_J_	_____	_____	_C_	neat and tidy
organized	_C_	_____	_____	_J_	disorganized

Example 4.7 _____

- **Title:** *Lily's Crossing*
- **Author:** Patricia Reilly Giff
- **Grade Level:** 4–6
- **Summary:** Lily, her father, and her grandmother go to their summer house on the Atlantic Coast every year. In the summer of 1944, how-

ever, life changes when World War II takes Lily's father overseas and Lily meets a Hungarian refugee who has lost much of his family.

Polar Opposites

Rate both Lily and Albert on each of the characteristics below. Put an "L" for Lily and an "A" for Albert.

dishonest	____	____	____	____	____	honest
cowardly	____	____	____	____	____	brave
weak	____	____	____	____	____	strong
dependent	____	____	____	____	____	independent
impulsive	____	____	____	____	____	thoughtful
self-centered	____	____	____	____	____	selfless

Polar opposites may be used successfully with all age groups to facilitate readers' reflection on characters. They offer a structure for discussions and encourage critical thinking as students analyze and synthesize what they know about a character in order to make judgments.

POWERFUL PASSAGES

The powerful passages activity (Yopp & Yopp, 2003) provides students with the opportunity to identify in a reading selection an excerpt that they find compelling, interesting, or in some way personally meaningful and to share it with their peers. After reading a text, each student revisits the literature and skims it for a short passage he or she wishes to share. There are, of course, no "correct, "incorrect," "good," or "poor" choices. Selections are a matter of personal appeal. Once each student has made a selection, students spend a few minutes in quiet rehearsal in preparation for reading aloud. Then students meet in pairs, read their passages to one another, and discuss the reasons for their choices. Students are given several opportunities to share their passages with different peers and, in turn, to listen to several peers' selections.

If everyone has read the same text, this activity provides a means for students to reexperience portions of the book together. Social interactions about passages enrich students' reflections on and responses to the book. Students notice commonalities and differences in their choices and gain insights into the thinking of their peers. Comprehension deepens as they listen and as they explain their reasons for and responses to their selection. Students' responses and explanations are often increasingly elaborated and sometimes revised as they share with additional partners.

This activity may also be used when students have read different texts, such as those read during a silent sustained reading period. Students select a passage from their respective books to share, rehearse it briefly, and then read it aloud to several different partners. Because students have a choice in what they share, the passages are discussed with personal commitment and enthusiasm, even passion. This enthusiasm can ignite the listeners' interest in the book.

The opportunity for rehearsal is particularly important for lower-achieving readers because it increases the likelihood of fluent oral reading. With rehearsal, reading aloud to peers is a successful and positive experience rather than an uncomfortable one, and this contributes to students' sense of competence.

An alternative to the oral sharing of personally selected quotations is a written sharing. Participants select a passage to share and copy it onto a piece of paper. These papers are then displayed around the classroom; the room becomes a gallery of quotations. The teacher and students circulate around the room to read the passages, carrying pencils so that they can write a response on any of the papers. Responses may be brief or lengthy and often take the form of comments such as "Oh, yes! I really enjoyed this part, too!" "I felt so bad when I read this part," "This was very funny! I like how the author spelled the words in the section to exaggerate the sounds," "Many of us selected this same passage!" "This really makes you think about how lucky you are and how much we don't know about other people in the world," "I was stunned when I read this section. It came so suddenly and was so unexpected. The book seemed so lighthearted at first, then changed with a few words." After the gallery walk, the group discusses the experience.

A variation on this open-choice activity is to ask students to peruse the text to locate passages of a particular type. Teachers may wish to have students return to the text to find a passage that conveys emotion, provides information about the setting or a character, or clarifies a concept. A more focused discussion of the author's language can then occur.

Occasionally teachers ask students to select a single sentence rather than a passage. Students share their "Significant Sentences" in the same way as described for the powerful passages activity.

LITERARY REPORT CARDS

Literary report cards provide student with a vehicle for analysis of characters. In this activity, suggested by Johnson and Louis (1987), students are given the opportunity to issue grades to characters in a reading selection. Initially, the teacher may select the "subjects" on which the characters will be graded. Rather than academic areas, characters may be graded on personality traits, such as "courageous" or "patient." Eventually, the students may generate the subject areas. Selection of subject areas requires higher-level thinking, as the students reflect on the character, analyze his or her qualities and behavior, and label the qualities. In addition to awarding the grades, students comment on or cite evidence for each grade. Report cards themselves may be modeled after real report cards used at the school that the students attend.

Example 4.8

- **Title:** *Frindle*
- **Author:** Andrew Clements
- **Grade Level:** 3–5
- **Summary:** Nick is a creative fifth-grader who is known as a bit of a troublemaker. He meets his match in Mrs. Granger, a strict language arts teacher who loves the dictionary. Nick causes much excitement with his invention of a new word—*frindle*—and gains national attention for the word and the trouble it causes at his school. Mrs. Granger is a great teacher and knows just what it takes to get students excited about words.

Literary Report Card

Student: Nicholas Allen		
	Grade	*Comment*
Language arts	*A*	*Nick wrote an excellent, detailed report on the history of words. He has great presentation skills. He invented a new word.*
Creativity	*A*	*Nick turned a classroom into a tropical island. He has inventive ideas for postponing homework assignments.*
Leadership skills	*A*	*Nick persuaded his classmates to use the word* frindle, *even though they would get in trouble.*
Obedience	*D*	*Nick's new word caused problems at school. He didn't stop using the word when the teacher asked him to stop.*
Generosity	*A*	*Nick established a scholarship in Mrs. Granger's name.*

Example 4.9 _____

- **Title:** *My Father's Dragon*
- **Author:** Ruth Stiles Gannett
- **Grade Level:** 2–4
- **Summary:** Elmer Elevator wishes to fly. When an alley cat tells him about a flying dragon that is being held captive on faraway Wild Island, Elmer runs away from home to rescue it. On the island, he meets many animals that try to interfere with his plans. He cleverly evades them all, frees the dragon, and they fly away together.

Literary Report Card

Airborne Elementary School		
Student: Elmer Elevator		
Characteristic	*Grade*	*Comment*
Kind	A	*Elmer befriends a cat and provides him with shelter and food.*
Adventurous	A	*Elmer wants to fly. He runs away to Wild Island.*
Obedient	D	*Elmer disobeys his mother. He runs away. He sneaks aboard a ship.*
Clever	A	*He is able to hide from the sailors. He finds a way to distract the animals on the island that try to eat him.*
Prepared	C	*Elmer takes a bag of supplies, but he doesn't carry enough food.*

For primary-grade students, descriptors such as "good," "satisfactory," and "needs to improve" may be more appropriate than letter grades.

Example 4.10 _____

- **Title:** *Nate the Great*
- **Author:** Marjorie Weinman Sharmat
- **Grade Level:** K–2
- **Summary:** Nate the Great is a detective whose job is to find a missing picture.

Literary Report Card

Gumshoe Elementary School		
Student: Nate		
G—Good S—Satisfactory N—Needs to Improve		
Area	**Grade**	**Comments**
Believes in himself	G	*He is sure that he can find Annie's lost picture.*
Can be counted on	G	*He leaves a note for his mother when he leaves the house. He takes his job very seriously.*
Is smart	G	*He makes a plan for finding the picture, figures that the only place Fang could bury something is in the backyard, knows red and yellow make orange, and finds the picture.*
Is patient	S	*He digs for two hours in the backyard but is in a hurry to leave Rosamond's house and gets mad when Harry paints him.*

Example 4.11 _____

- **Title:** *The Tale of Peter Rabbit*
- **Author:** Beatrix Potter
- **Grade Level:** K–2
- **Summary:** Peter Rabbit disobeys his mother and goes to Mr. McGregor's garden. There he is chased by Mr. McGregor and barely escapes.

Literary Report Card

O'Hare Private School		
Student: Peter		
G—Good S—Satisfactory N—Needs to Improve		
Area	**Grade**	**Comments**
Obedience	N	*He went to Mr. McGregor's garden even though his mother told him not to.*
Bravery	N	*He cried a lot when he got caught in a net and when he couldn't find his way out of the garden.*
Sports	G	*He ran fast, jumped into a bucket and out of a window, and wiggled under a fence.*

Any grade given by the student should be accepted as long as he or she is able to provide a reason for the grade. In Example 4.11, some students may give Peter Rabbit an "S" or a "G" in bravery rather than an "N," stating that he was brave to go into McGregor's garden. It is important that the teacher be open to a range of responses and focus on the students' abilities to provide reasonable, thoughtful explanations for the grades they award.

All graded areas should be stated in the positive form. It makes no sense to award a character an "A" in impatience, for example, or a "D" in dishonesty.

PLOT PROFILES

In a plot profile (Johnson & Louis, 1987; see also DeGroff & Galda, 1992), students identify the main events in a story and then rate the events along some scale, such as level of excitement or impact on the character. Events are numbered, and these numbers are placed along a horizontal axis, as in Example 4.12. The rating for each event is plotted along the vertical axis. Lines are drawn between each point, thus creating a line graph. Johnson and Louis have suggested that when students rate events in terms of their excitement, they use the following scale: "Calm," "Very Interesting," "Exciting," "WOW!"

Example 4.12 _____

- **Title:** *Number the Stars*
- **Author:** Lois Lowry
- **Grade Level:** 4–6
- **Summary:** This is the story of one family's efforts to help save Danish Jews from the Nazis.

Events

1. *Running home from school, Ellen, Annemarie, and Kirsti are stopped by German soldiers.*

2. *Peter visits after curfew and tells the family that Germans are ordering stores run by Jews closed.*

3. *Ellen comes to stay with the Johansens when her parents flee.*

4. *The soldiers search the Johansen apartment for the Rosen family. They challenge Ellen because of her dark hair.*

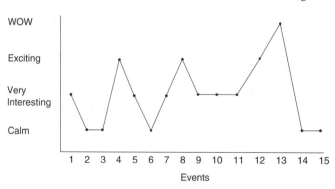

5. *Mrs. Johansen, Annemarie, Ellen, and Kirsti travel to Uncle Henrik's.*

6. *The girls play at Uncle Henrik's.*

7. *"Aunt Bertie's" loved ones gather around her casket.*

8. *The soldiers interrupt the gathering.*

9. *Peter organizes the Jews to head to the boat.*

10. *Mrs. Johansen leaves with the Rosens.*

11. *Annemarie sees her mother on the ground and helps her to the house.*

12. *Annemarie races through the woods to deliver the envelope to Henrik.*

13. *Annemarie is stopped and questioned by soldiers. They discover the package.*

14. *Uncle Henrik explains the Resistance and the handkerchief to Annemarie.*

15. *The war ends. Annemarie learns the truth about Lise's death.*

An alternative to a line graph is a cut-and-paste grid. Students write, and perhaps illustrate, key events from the story on separate pieces of paper. Students paste these events higher or lower on a large butcher paper grid, depending on the ratings they give. The key events and ratings shown in the line graph in Example 4.12 are depicted in the cut-and-paste format in Example 4.13. Students may work individually or collaboratively in small groups on plot profiles, coming to consensus on story events and ratings. If other individuals or groups of students are reading the same book, plot profiles may be compared. Teachers should expect differences between individual or group selections of key events and ratings.

Example 4.13

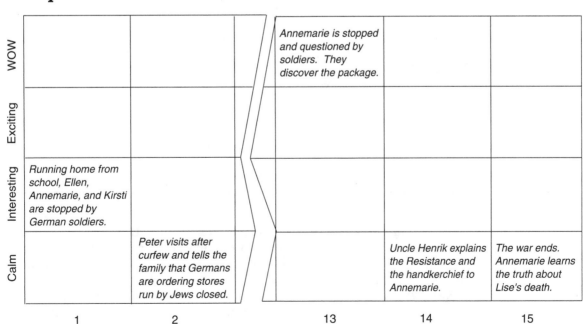

	1	2	13	14	15
WOW			Annemarie is stopped and questioned by soldiers. They discover the package.		
Exciting					
Interesting	Running home from school, Ellen, Annemarie, and Kirsti are stopped by German soldiers.				
Calm		Peter visits after curfew and tells the family that Germans are ordering stores run by Jews closed.		Uncle Henrik explains the Resistance and the handkerchief to Annemarie.	The war ends. Annemarie learns the truth about Lise's death.

Events

VENN DIAGRAMS

Venn diagrams, named for the nineteenth-century British logician John Venn, offer a means for students to compare and contrast two or more characters, settings, or other information in a work of literature. Venn diagrams provide graphic representations, in the form of overlapping circles, of features that are unique and common to selected topics. The readers draw two or more overlapping circles and label each circle. Where the circles overlap, features common to the topics are listed, and where they do not overlap, features unique to each topic are recorded. Example 4.14 displays a Venn diagram comparing and contrasting fruit bats and birds from the book *Stellaluna,* by Janell Cannon.

Example 4.14 _____

- **Title:** *Stellaluna*
- **Author:** Janell Cannon
- **Grade Level:** K-3
- **Summary:** A fruit bat is cared for by a family of birds after falling from its mother's grasp while fleeing an owl. The bat and birds find that even though they are different, they are alike.

Venn Diagram

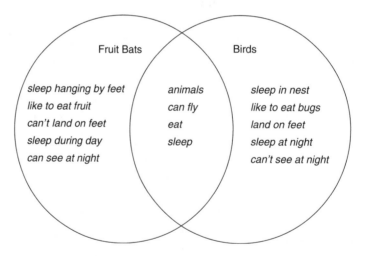

Fruit Bats | Birds

Fruit Bats	animals	Birds
sleep hanging by feet	*animals*	*sleep in nest*
like to eat fruit	*can fly*	*like to eat bugs*
can't land on feet	*eat*	*land on feet*
sleep during day	*sleep*	*sleep at night*
can see at night		*can't see at night*

Comparisions can also be made across books, thus moving the students beyond "local reading" (Wolf in Hartman & Hartman, 1993)—a focus on individual works of literature with little or no effort to make connections across texts. For instance, the perspectives and actions of Johnny in *Johnny Tremain* by Esther Forbes can be compared and contrasted with those of Tim in *My Brother Sam Is Dead* by James Lincoln Collier and Christopher Collier. Each of these characters is a boy who lives during the time of the American Revolution. The lives and works of Sojourner Truth and Cesar Chavez can be examined in Example 4.15, and similarities and differences in *Adam of the Road* by Elizabeth Janet Gray, *The Door in the Wall* by Marguerite de Angeli, and *Crispin: The Cross of Lead* by Avi can be explored through the Venn diagram shown in Figure 4.16.

Example 4.15 _____

- **Titles:** *Only Passing Through: The Story of Sojourner Truth* (Anne Rockwell)

   Harvesting Hope: The Story of Cesar Chavez (Kathleen Krull)

- **Grade Level:** K–6

- **Summaries:** Each of these books describes an individual who became a champion of justice. Sojourner Truth was a slave who gained her freedom and traveled around the countryside to spread the truth about the conditions of slaves. Cesar Chavez, a migrant worker, organized peaceful protests and improved the lives of thousands.

Venn Diagram

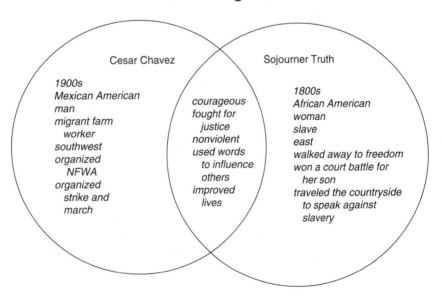

Example 4.16 _____

- **Titles:** *Adam of the Road* (Elizabeth Janet Gray)

   Crispin: The Cross of Lead (Avi)

   The Door in the Wall (Marguerite de Angeli)

- **Grade Level:** 5–8

- **Summary:** Each of these books details the experiences of a boy growing up during the Middle Ages.

Venn Diagram

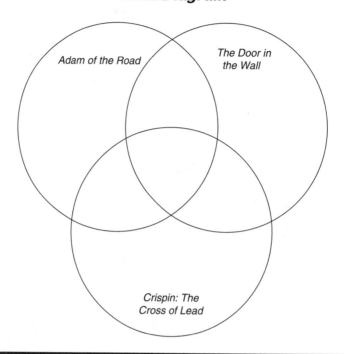

Readers can use Venn diagrams to compare themselves to a character. In Example 4.17, students can compare their lifestyles to that of a young boy whose people have a Stone Age way of life.

Example 4.17 _____

- **Title:** *Lobo of the Tasaday*
- **Author:** John Nance
- **Grade Level:** 2–5
- **Summary:** Lobo is a young member of the Tasaday, a group of people who live in a rain forest on an island in the southern Philippines. The author tells the true story of their Stone Age lifestyle and their discovery by the modern world in 1971.

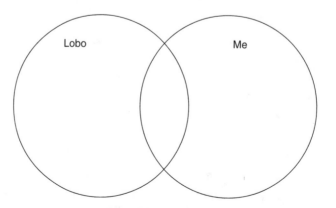

BOOK CHARTS

Book charts provide another structure for students to make connections across books. Through the use of book charts, students can discover patterns in literature, identify conventions in various genres, deepen and extend understandings of issues or concepts, and come to recognize the universality of certain themes. Students can compare and contrast characters' experiences and their responses to those experiences and analyze similarities and differences in plots. Through this activity, students' roles as readers are expanded beyond "the boundaries of a single text" (Hartman & Hartman, 1993, p. 202).

If all students in a class or group have read or listened to several of the same books, together they may develop a large chart on butcher paper that captures information from the books in a number of categories. If small groups of students have read different books that focus on the same topic or have a similar theme, then each group may contribute information about its book to a class chart.

A book chart that focuses on "the immigrant experience" may be developed when students have read *In the Year of the Boar and Jackie Robinson* by Bette Lord, *Dragonwings* by Laurence Yep, and *Journey to America* by Sonia Levitin. Categories on the chart may include book title, author, character, native country, positive experiences, and negative or challenging experiences.

"Survival" could be the focus of a book chart if students have read *The Sign of the Beaver* by Elizabeth George Speare, *Island of the Blue Dolphins* by Scott O'Dell, *Hatchet* by Gary Paulsen, and *Julie of the Wolves* by Jean Craighead George. In each of these books, the protagonist is stranded alone and must demonstrate resourcefulness and courage in order to survive. Categories for this book chart may include author, title, reasons the protagonist is alone, internal challenges, external challenges, and outcome.

Sylvester and the Magic Pebble by William Steig, *The Magic Fish* by Freya Littledale, and *The Three Wishes* by M. Jean Craig each have a character in the story who is granted wishes. Students may record the title, author, wishes made, and the consequences of the wishes for each of these books. Students may also include wishes they would make given the opportunity. Thus, book charts can prompt both efferent and aesthetic responses.

We share two book charts in Examples 4.18 and 4.19. On any book chart, a column in which students record their feelings, reactions, or book ratings also may be included. This column will invite students to share their responses to the literature.

Western (1980) has described a book chart in which students compare the characters, settings, problems, and endings of three versions of "Jack and the Beanstalk" and analyze their similarities and differences. A framework for this type of book chart using three versions of the "Cinderella" story is provided in Example 4.20.

Book charts may be developed by individuals, small groups of students, or the entire class. Teachers of younger students will likely play a greater role in facilitating classroom discussions and in recording information.

Example 4.18

- ■ **Focus:** Name and Identity

Book Chart

Title	*Author*	*Grade Level*	*Protagonist(s)*	*Threat to Identity*	*Resolution*
My Name Is Maria Isabel	*Alma Flor Ada*	*3–4*	*Maria Isabel*	*Her teacher calls her Mary because there are two Marias in the class already.*	*Maria uses a writing assignment to express her greatest wish: to be called by her own name. The teacher does so.*
When My Name was Keoko	*Linda Sue Park*	*4–6*	*Sun-hee Tae-yul*	*The Japanese who occupy South Korea demand that Koreans take on Japanese names.*	*Sun-hee, Tae-yul, and their family keep their heritage alive in their hearts. The war ends and Korea is freed.*
My Name Is Yoon	*Helen Recorvits*	*1–3*	*Yoon*	*A Korean-immigrant to the U.S. is asked to write her name using the alphabet rather than the characters with which she is familiar.*	*Yoon recognizes that however her name is written, she is still Yoon.*
The Name Jar	*Yangsook Choi*	*1–3*	*Unhei*	*A new immigrant to the U.S. is worried that classmates will tease her about her Korean name. She considers suggestions for an American name.*	*Unhei decides to to keep her own name.*

Example 4.19

- ■ **Focus:** Overcoming Loss
- ■ **Grade Level:** 4–8

Book Chart

Title	*Author*	*Summary*	*The Loss*	*Dealing with the Loss*
Love That Dog	*Sharon Creech*	*With the encouragement of his teacher, a boy uses poetry to express his feelings about the death of his dog.*	*Dog*	*Through writing poetry*

Title	Author	Summary	The Loss	Dealing with the Loss
Out of the Dust	Karen Hesse	Billie Jo's mother and baby brother die tragically, and Billie Jo's hands are scarred by fire.	Mother, baby brother, and use of hands	By living one day at a time and by forgiving her father and herself
Locomotion	Jacqueline Woodson	Lonnie Collins Motion's life changes when his parents die in a fire and he and his sister are sent to separate foster homes. A teacher helps him express his feelings and memories in free verse.	Parents and sister	Through writing poetry

Example 4.20

- **Titles:** *Yeh-Shen: A Cinderella Story from China* (Ai-Ling Louie)

  Moss Gown (William H. Hooks)

  The Egyptian Cinderella (Shirley Climo)
- **Grade Level:** 2–5

Book Chart

	Yeh-Shen	Moss Gown	The Egyptian Cinderella	Similarities	Differences	Conclusions
Characters						
Setting						
Problem						
Ending						

Another type of book chart is the inquiry chart, or I-chart (Hoffman, 1992). As can be seen in Example 4.21, students record questions they have about a topic and anything they already know related to the questions. Then the students consult a variety of sources and record their findings on the chart. At the bottom of the chart, students summarize information. Students must compare information across texts and sometimes reconcile conflicting data in order to complete their summaries.

Example 4.21

■ **Grade Level:** 2–4

I-Chart

Topic: *Frogs*	*What Is Their Habitat?*	*What Do They Eat?*	*What Preys on Them?*	*Other Interesting Facts*	*New Questions*
What we know					
It's a Frog's Life (Steve Parker)					
Very First Things to Know about Frogs (Patricia Grossman)					
The Frog (Paul Starosta)					
Frogs (Gail Gibbons)					
Summary					

It has been argued that opportunities for narrow reading—reading several texts by the same author or on the same topic—benefit English learners (Krashen, 2004; Peregoy & Boyle, 2005; Schmitt & Carter, 2000). An author's distinctive style, word and phrasing choices, and use of certain expressions become familiar to readers, and so reading the second or third book by an author is easier than reading the first. Similarly, books on the same topic have overlapping vocabulary, concepts, and structures. Each book read on a topic supports the comprehensibility of the next. The more familiar students are with the language and the content of a topic, the more easily students can read books on the topic. Book charts and I-charts offer students the opportunity for narrow reading.

Struggling readers experience the same advantages when reading multiple books by the same author or on the same topic. Their successful comprehension of texts will serve to motivate additional reading, which, in turn, supports reading development. Although it is important to read widely, jumping from one genre to another, one topic to another, or one discourse style to another with little opportunity for extended reading on the same topic or in the same genre gives struggling readers little chance to build comfort and competence with text. Exposure to the same concepts phrased or elaborated on differently across texts and repetition of key vocabulary across texts builds students' background knowledge and language, enabling them to have more successful interactions with text.

POETIC RESPONSES

Writing poetry in response to literature can be a powerful exercise that allows students to express their understandings and feelings about a reading selection and that develops a sense of pride in students as they become authors whose words can move others. In three types of poetic responses—Found poems, I Am poems, and Where I'm From poems—students capture in free verse what they feel is the essence of a selection.

Found poems are arrangements of language that has been selected from, or "found" in, a reading selection (Dunning & Stafford, 1992). After reading, students return to the text to identify words and phrases that are appealing, important, or meaningful. Each student records words and phrases of his or her choice and then arranges them to form a poem. Students try several arrangements of the words and phrases until they create one that satisfies them.

Found poems encourage students to reflect on and examine the language of the author and to shift the language from one genre (the genre of the original source) to another (poetry). What phrases in the text evoke strong images or emotions in the reader? What words are unusual, highly relevant, interesting, or telling? What words or phrases summarize the author's intent? How can these words and phrases be used in another way to share reactions to or perceptions of the author's work? Readers select any words and phrases they wish and then organize the language in whatever way suits them. Because students draw entirely from the language of the author, the linguistic demands on the students are lessened. Yet, because students must examine the author's language in order to make choices for use in their own poetry, they engage with rich language. The scaffolding provides support and the close attention to and use of the author's language provides an opportunity for language development. Thus, Found poems are beneficial for all students, including English learners. Examples 4.22 and 4.23 are poems "found" by students in the language of works of fiction and nonfiction, respectively.

I Am poems (adapted from Fisher & Frey, 2003) provide students with a frame for building a poem. Students choose a character in a reading selection and revisit the text to think about the experiences, thoughts, and qualities of the character. Students may be encouraged to brainstorm or create a character web (described in Chapter Three) in preparation for writing the poem. Then, students complete each line in the poem ("I am . . .," "I feel . . .," "I wish . . .," and so on), responding in the voice of the character. Lines are rearranged in whatever way appeals to the poet. The underlined phrases in Examples 4.24 are a fourth-grade student's words as she completed each line after reading *The Year of Miss Agnes,* by Kirkpatrick Hill. Example 4.25 provides two I Am poems in response to Jack London's *The Call of the Wild,* each written from a different character's perspective.

Where I'm From poems also provide a scaffold for students' writing in response to a reading selection. Based on a poem by George Ella Lyon (Lyon, 1999) in which the refrain "I am from" is repeated as the poet describes elements of her heritage and life, and adapted from Christensen (2000), who had her students write about their lives using the poem as a model, the Where I'm From poem can be used to capture the voice, experiences, and feelings of a character in a story or in a contemporary or historical figure in a biography. Example 4.26 shares two students' poems in response to *Out of the Dust,* by Karen Hesse.

Each of these three types of poetry provides a scaffold for student writing. In the Found poem, students draw entirely on the language of the author, and in the I Am and Where I'm From poems, students are provided frames on which to build their poems. Thus, all students—including reluctant writers—can find writing poetry in response to literature a highly successful experience that enriches their understandings of the reading selections.

Example 4.22 _____

- **Title:** *Virgie Goes to School with Us Boys*
- **Author:** Elizabeth Fitzgerald Howard
- **Grade Level:** K–3
- **Summary:** After President Lincoln's Emancipation Proclamation, former slaves were allowed to attend school. Virgie's brothers walk seven miles to a school opened by the Quakers, and Virgie, a girl, is determined to attend as well. Based on a real family's history, the author is the granddaughter of one of Virgie's brothers.

Found Poem

Virgie always asking,
"Can I go to school?"

Too little.
Scarcely big as a field mouse.
Girls don't need school.

She kept asking and asking.

Too little.
Scarcely big as a field mouse.
Girls don't need school.

Virgie always asking.

All free people
　need learning.
You can go to school with the boys.
Free.

Example 4.23 _____

- **Title:** *I Face the Wind*
- **Author:** Vicki Cobb
- **Grade Level:** 1–3
- **Summary:** In this Robert F. Siebert Honor Book, the author provides information about the wind and suggests activities that help children understand scientific concepts.

Found Poem

Student 1:

Strong wind
You can't see
You can feel
This force that's pushing you.
Air is real stuff.
Molecules—gazillions of moving
　air molecules.
The push of the wind.

Student 2:

Your hair blows.
You lose your hat!
Why?
Air is real stuff.
Air is heavier than nothing.
Experiment. Imagine.
Can you feel it?
Yay!

Example 4.24 _____

- **Title:** *The Year of Miss Agnes*
- **Author:** Kirkpatrick Hill
- **Grade Level:** 2–5
- **Summary:** Frederika and her classmates in a one-room schoolhouse in remote Alaska find that their new teacher is very different from the others who have come and gone so quickly. She wears pants, shares music, reads stories aloud, and finds the strengths in each of her students. She also insists that Frederika's deaf sister attend school. Readers get a glimpse of Alaska's geography, history, and culture.

I Am Poem

I am *Frederika*.
I want *to go to school*.
I wonder *who our new teacher will be*.
I hear *music from her record player*.
I see *a woman in pants*!
I am *Frederika*.
I pretend *I am from another time*.
I feel *I am inside the book she reads*.
I touch *the big map on the wall*.
I worry *our teacher will hate the smell of fish*.
I cry *when I think about her leaving us*.
I am *Frederika*.
I understand *why I must learn arithmetic*.
I say *my sister is deaf*.
I dream *that I will see the world*.
I try *not to cry*.
I hope *our teacher will stay*.
I am *Fred*.

Example 4.25

- **Title:** *The Call of the Wild*
- **Author:** Jack London
- **Grade Level:** 5–8
- **Summary:** Buck is a well-cared-for family dog who is removed from his comfortable home in California to serve as a sled dog in the Alaskan wilderness. John Thornton, a prospector, becomes his master.

I Am Poem

I am *John Thornton*.
I wonder *why Buck goes away for a long time*.
I hear *wolves howling*.
I see *a valley filled with gold*.
I want *to become rich*.
I am *John Thornton*.
I pretend *to fight my dog*.
I feel *calloused hands*.
I touch *yellow gold*.
I worry *that my dog will get hurt*.
I cry *when my leg gets hurt from the snow*.
I am *John Thornton*.
I understand *my dog*.
I say *"You devil."*
I dream *of being rich*.
I try *to become rich*.

I hope *to be successful*.
I am *John Thornton*.

I am *Buck*.
I wonder *why the snow falls*.
I hear *wolves howling*.
I see *snow*.
I want *a loving master*.
I am *Buck*.
I pretend *to be a wolf sometimes*.
I feel *the cold snow*.
I touch *the hard ground*.
I worry *about my master leaving me*.
I cry *to the heavens*.
I am *Buck*.
I understand *the call of the wild*.
I say *"Bark!"*
I dream *about cavemen*.
I try *to help my master*.
I hope *to catch a moose and eat it*.
I am *Buck*.

Example 4.26 _____

- ■ **Title:** *Out of the Dust*
- ■ **Author:** Karen Hesse
- ■ **Grade Level:** 4–6
- ■ **Summary:** Thirteen-year-old Billie Jo experiences the Depression and the dust storms that ravage Oklahoma and the Dust Bowl during the 1930s. In a tragic accident, her mother and infant brother die and Billie Jo and her father ultimately find their way toward one another.

Where I'm From Poem

Student 1:

I am from wheat fields, from farmland
 From a little house, a tractor, and apple trees.

I am from a redheaded daddy, a man of the sod, who always wanted a
 boy.
And a Ma, a Ma who lies on the hill.

I am from the piano, from moving my fingers across the keys
 From rhythm, from music, from a Ma who played and
 Taught me to play.

I am from dust so thick we cannot see, we cannot breathe,
 Tearing up the fields
From waves and waves
And waves of dust

From days and days of dust.
And drought.
Again.

I am from horror, from grief so deep I feel everything and nothing,
*   from emptiness, from terrible pain.*
I am from kerosene by the stove, from fire.
I am from a dead mother and a dead brother.
I am from a silent, distant father.

I am from scarred hands, a scarred land, a scarred life, scarred love.

I am from guilt. I am from anger.
I am from running away and finding nowhere to go.

I am from forgiveness and from hope.

I am from this land.

Student 2:

I am from dust and dust

And dust
I am from wind and drought
I am from death.

I am from accidents and fire that destroys so much outside of me and
Inside of me.
I am from loneliness and pain.

I am from the farmlands of Oklahoma.
This is where I belong.

SKETCH TO STRETCH

Sketch to stretch offers readers an opportunity to think about and share what a text means to them as they recast their understandings from one symbol system, text, into a different symbol system, a sketch (Harste, Short, & Burke, 1988; Short, Kauffman, & Kahn, 2000; Whitin, 2002). By asking students to represent linguistic understandings in a nonlinguistic manner, teachers support students in thinking about, making connections to, elaborating on, and interpreting text. In addition, readers become more aware of whether they understand a text; comprehension monitoring is facilitated.

In sketch to stretch, students first listen to or read a text or portion of a text. The teacher then prompts them to sketch what the text means to them. They are encouraged to share through lines, colors, shapes, and pictures what they understand or feel about the ideas in the text. They show their sketches to small groups of peers who offer interpretations. After listening to the interpretations of peers, each artist explains his or her sketch. According to Whitin (2002), the sharing and explaining of the sketches provides students with an opportunity to revisit the text through literary discussions and to appreciate diverse perspectives of a text.

Although some students will sketch in silence, Whitin has recommended that the students be permitted to talk to one another as they sketch if they choose. In her experience, students build on each other's ideas about a text as they sketch and come to understand that by collaborating they can construct meaningful interpretations and extend their ideas.

In Example 4.27, two fifth-grade students responded to *Grandfather's Journey,* by Allen Say. One student shared that her sketch shows that Grandfather is in two places. "There is the ocean and the big farm field on one side, which is California, and on the other side, there are mountains, which is Japan. The line down the middle shows that he is in two places." The second student drew a picture that shows that Grandfather's heart is divided between his two countries.

Example 4.27 _____

- **Title:** *Grandfather's Journey*
- **Author:** Allen Say
- **Grade Level:** K–6
- **Summary:** A Japanese American man tells the story of his grandfather's move to America and of his feelings of love and longing for both his native country and his adopted country.

Sample Sketches

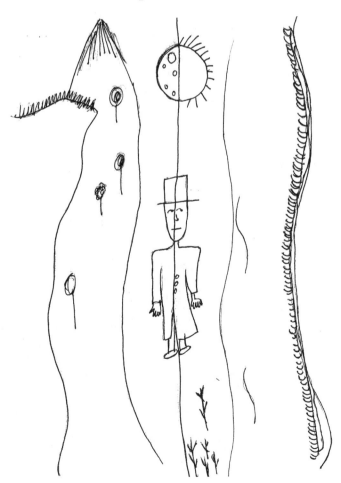

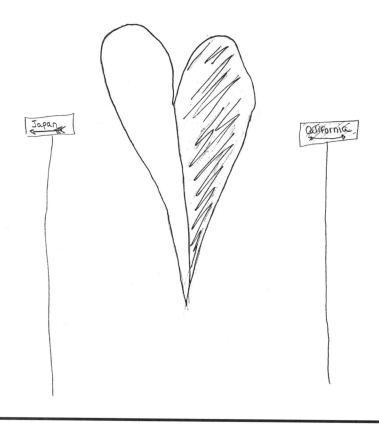

Short, Kauffman, and Kahn (2000) note that sketch to stretch not only supports responses to a text as a whole but can also be used to help students think about a particular issue in a text. For example, if students want to discuss how Grandfather felt when he first saw the desert rock formations, farm fields, mountains, and rivers of the New World, they might create sketches that capture those feelings.

Although intended for use with students who have read or listened to the same book, sketch to stretch is also a valuable activity when students have read different texts. After a sustained silent reading time, for example, the teacher might ask students to sketch what the text they are reading means to them at this moment in time. Students sketch, then meet with peers who consider the sketch and generate ideas about the text and what the sketch means. Then the artist shares the text and explains the sketch. Students articulate their reasons for symbols, colors, lines, and so forth in their sketches, and they have an authentic reason to provide a brief summary of their reading selections. Further, students' interest in a peer's text may be piqued as they view the sketch and engage in discussion. Such social interactions about books are motivating, and students place "a high priority on reading books they hear about from others" (Palmer, Codling, & Gambrell, 1994, p. 177).

Sketch to stretch is effectively used with students of diverse reading and language proficiency levels. Sophisticated ideas may be represented in the students' sketches that otherwise might not be communicated verbally. The discussions that ensue provide an opportunity for language and cognitive development as students converse with one another, clarifying and extending language and meaning in a personal and purposeful communicative context.

3-D RESPONSES

Like sketching, creating a three-dimensional representation of a reading selection provides students with a nonverbal medium for responding to literature and challenges students to process text deeply. Subsequent discussions support and extend comprehension and language development. When students are reading different books, their interest in new selections may be sparked.

Many materials can be manipulated and shaped into 3-D representations, including clay, playdough, straws, and pipe cleaners. One of our favorite materials is foil. After reading, students are provided a foil sheet of approximately 12 by 12 inches and asked to create a sculpture that captures an idea, feeling, event, character, or key point in the recently read selection. Students bend, twist, and tear the foil to serve their needs. This creative process may take anywhere from three to fifteen minutes.

After students have completed their foil creations, they turn to one or two neighbors to share. Classmates may be asked what they see in the work before the sculptor shares his or her thinking, or the sculptor of the piece may explain it immediately. Questions, clarifications, and elaborations are encouraged. Next, students may circulate around the classroom to examine all the foil creations, stopping and talking with one another as they circulate. Students are often intrigued by their peers' representations, and when all students have read the same book, they gain an appreciation for the variety of personal responses to a text.

The hands-on nature of this activity supports English learners in particular because a nonverbal medium is used to communicate responses to a reading selection, and students listen and speak to peers about their creations in pairs or small groups. The physical product provides an additional source of input and a context for language as students point to, manipulate, and use their creations in their conversations.

CONCLUSION

Postreading activities are useful for enhancing students' comprehension of, personal responses to, connections with, and appreciation of literature. Polar opposites and literary report cards provide interesting and motivating formats for thinking about and analyzing characters. Powerful passages allows all students to identify, share, and respond to passages they find compelling in the literature. Plot profiles, Venn diagrams, and book charts offer means for summarizing, organizing, analyzing, and synthesizing information. Poetic responses, sketch to stretch, and 3-D responses invite students to creatively express their understandings, interpretations, and responses to the literature.

REFERENCES

Ada, A. F. (1993). *My name is Maria Isabel.* New York: Atheneum.

Avi. (2002). *Crispin: The cross of lead.* New York: Hyperion.

Cannon, J. (1993). *Stellaluna.* San Diego, CA: Harcourt Brace.

Choi, Y. (2001). *The name jar.* New York: Knopf.

Christensen, L. (2000). *Reading, writing, and rising up: Teaching about social justice and the power of the word.* Milwaukee, WI: Rethinking Schools Ltd.

Clements, A. (1998). *Frindle.* New York: Aladdin.

Climo, S. (1989). *The Egyptian Cinderella.* New York: Thomas Y. Crowell.

Cobb, V. (2003). *I face the wind.* HarperCollins.

Collier, J. L., & Collier, C. (1974). *My brother Sam is dead.* New York: Four Winds.

Craig, M. J. (1968). *The three wishes.* New York: Scholastic.

Creech. S. (2001). *Love that dog.* New York: HarperCollins.

Curtis, C. P. (1995). *The Watsons go to Birmingham—1963.* New York: Bantam Doubleday Dell.

de Angeli, M. (1949). *The door in the wall.* New York: Scholastic.

deGroff, L., & Galda, L. (1992). Responding to literature: Activities for exploring books. In B. Cullinan (Ed.), *Invitation to read: More children's literature in the reading program.* Newark, DE: International Reading Association.

Dunning, S., & Stafford, W. (1992). *Getting the knack: 20 poetry writing exercises.* Urbana, IL: National Council of Teachers of English.

Fisher, D., & Frey, N. (2003). Writing instruction for struggling adolescent readers: A gradual release model. *Journal of Adolescent and Adult Literacy, 46,* 396–405.

Forbes, E. (1971). *Johnny Tremain.* New York: Dell.

Frost, R. (1959). *You come too.* New York: Holt, Rinehart, & Winston.

Gannett, R. S. (1948). *My father's dragon.* New York: Random House.

George, J. C. (1972). *Julie of the wolves.* New York: Harper & Row.

Gibbons, G. (1993). *Frogs.* New York: Holiday House.

Giff, P. R. (1997). *Lily's crossing.* New York: Delacorte.

Gray, E. J. (1942). *Adam of the road.* New York: Puffin.

Grossman, P. (1999). *Very first things to know about frogs.* New York: Workman.

Harste, J. C., Short, K. G., & Burke, C. (1988). *Creating classrooms for authors.* Portsmouth: NH: Heinemann.

Hartman, D. K., & Hartman, J. A. (1993). Reading across texts: Expanding the role of the reader. *The Reading Teacher, 47,* 202–211.

Hesse, K. (1997). *Out of the dust.* New York: Scholastic.

Hill, K. (2000). *The year of Miss Agnes.* New York: Aladdin.

Hoffman, J. V. (1992). Critical reading/thinking across the curriculum. Using I-charts to support learning. *Language Arts, 69,* 121–127.

Hoffman, M. (1991). *Amazing Grace.* New York: Dial.

Hooks, W. (1987). *Moss gown.* New York: Clarion Books.

Howard, E. F. (2000). *Virgie goes to school with us boys.* New York: Simon & Schuster.

Johnson, T., & Louis, D. (1987). *Literacy through literature.* Portsmouth, NH: Heinemann.

Konigsburg, E. L. (1974). *From the mixed-up files of Mrs. Basil E. Frankweiler.* New York: Dell.

Krashen, S. (2004). The case for narrow reading. *Language Magazine, 3* (5), 17–19.

Krull, K. (2003). *Harvesting hope: The story of Cesar Chavez.* San Diego, CA: Harcourt.

Leaf, M. (1967). *The story of Ferdinand.* New York: Scholastic.

Levitin, S. (1971). *Journey to America.* New York: Atheneum.

Littledale, F. (1986). *The magic fish.* New York: Scholastic.

London, J. (1974). *Call of the wild.* New York: Simon & Schuster.

Lord, B. (1984). *In the year of the boar and Jackie Robinson.* New York: Harper Junior Books.

Louie, A. L. (1982). *Yeh-Shen: A Cinderella story from China.* New York: Philomel.

Lowry, L. (1989). *Number the stars.* New York: Dell.

Lyon, G. E. (1999). *Where I'm from: Where poems come from.* Spring, TX: Absey.

Martin, A. M. (2002). *A corner of the universe.* New York: Scholastic.

Nance, J. (1982). *Lobo of the Tasaday.* New York: Pantheon.

O'Dell, S. (1960). *Island of the Blue Dolphins.* Boston: Houghton Mifflin.

Palmer, B. M., Codling, R. M., & Gambrell, L. B. (1994). In their own words: What elementary students have to say about motivation to read. *The Reading Teacher, 48,* 176–178.

Park, L. S. (2002). *When my name was Keoko.* New York: Dell Yearling.

Parker, S. (1999). *It's a frog's life.* Pleasantville, NY: Reader's Digest Children's Books.

Paulsen, G. (1987). *Hatchet.* New York: The Trumpet Club.

Peregoy, S. F., & Boyle, O. F. (2005). *Reading, writing, and learning in ESL.* Boston: Pearson.

Potter, B. (1989). *The tale of Peter Rabbit.* London: Penguin.

Recorvits, H. (2003). *My name is Yoon.* New York: Frances Foster.

Rockwell, A. (2000). *Only passing through: The story of Sojourner Truth.* New York: Dell Dragonfly.

Say, A. (1993). *Grandfather's journey.* New York: Houghton Mifflin.

Schmitt, N., & Carter, R. (2000). The lexical advantages of narrow reading for second language learners. *TESOL Journal, 9* (1), 4–9.

Sharmat, M. W. (1977). *Nate the great.* New York: Dell.

Short, K. G., Kauffman, G., & Kahn, L. H. (2000). "I just need to draw": Responding to literature across multiple sign systems. *The Reading Teacher, 54,* 160–171.

Speare, E. G. (1983). *The sign of the beaver.* Boston: Houghton Mifflin.

Starosta, P. (1996). *The frog.* Watertown, MA: Charlesbridge.

Steig, W. (1969). *Sylvester and the magic pebble.* New York: Simon & Schuster.

Western, L. (1980). A comparative study of literature through folk tale variants. *Language Arts, 57,* 395–402.

Whitin, P. (2002). Leading into literature circles through the sketch-to-stretch strategy. *The Reading Teacher, 55,* 444–454.

Woodson, J. (2003). *Locomotion.* New York: Grosset & Dunlap.

Yep, L. (1975). *Dragonwings.* New York: Harper Junior Books.

Yopp, R. H., & Yopp, H. K. (2003). Time with text. *The Reading Teacher, 57,* 284–287.

CHAPTER FIVE

Bookmaking

Bookmaking

Purposes

- To motivate students to read and write
- To creatively express and extend understandings of text
- To promote problem solving and decision making
- To provide a means for sharing
- To promote language development
- To promote an appreciation of reading and writing as personally meaningful, communicative acts

Activities

- Pop-up books
- Accordion books
- Fold-up books
- Upside-down books
- Retelling picture books
- Graduated-pages books
- Baggie books

Publishing student books in the classroom is a natural extension of reading books and a wonderful way to integrate the language arts. Bookmaking allows students to creatively express and extend their understandings of literature. It prompts children to revisit and reconsider the literature as they make decisions about their writing. It provides a forum for sharing their thinking with peers. It supports thoughtful and deliberate use of language to express ideas. And, it moves students toward a deeper understanding of writing and reading as exciting, personally meaningful, communicative acts.

When developing books in response to literature, students may summarize or retell the original work or borrow the author's literary structure to create a new work (Lancia, 1997). Summarization and retelling require students to identify important events or ideas for inclusion in their books and to make decisions about organizing information over a series of pages. The reconstruction of a story has been found to increase comprehension (Brown, 1975) and enhance students' concept of story structure and their language (Koskinen, Gambrell, Kapinus, & Heathington, 1988; Morrow, 1985).

An alternative to summarization and retelling is literary borrowing. One example of literary borrowing is patterned writing, in which the author's literary structure, or pattern, provides a scaffold for writing an original work. Predictable books serve as excellent models for patterned writing. A book that follows a repetitious pattern, such as *Over in the Meadow*, retold by John Lanstaff, is ideal. In this book, the author describes ten meadow animals. The rhythm and use of rhyme remain the same throughout the story. The students may change the setting and the animals in the story to create their own books, while maintaining the author's patterns. For example, they may write *Over in the Forest* or *Over in the Desert*. This will be especially interesting if the students are studying habitats in science.

The repetition in *The Little Red Hen,* by Vera Southgate, is also easily modeled. Students select an activity other than the making of bread, such as the baking of cupcakes, and identify and list the steps required in performing that activity. Then they use the language and structure of *The Little Red Hen* to develop their story. In addition, the students might provide different characters, such as relatives or friends. Each responds with "Not I," following the pattern established by the author.

The House That Jack Built, by David Cutts, and *I Know an Old Lady,* by Rose Bonne, both of which follow cumulative patterns, are excellent choices for modeling, as are *Chicken Soup with Rice,* by Maurice Sendak, and *The Very Hungry Caterpillar,* by Eric Carle, which follow sequence patterns.

Many works of nonfiction, too, provide a structure that can be borrowed. *I Didn't Know That Crocodiles Yawn to Keep Cool,* by Kate Petty, begins each page with the phrase "I didn't know that . . ." Individuals or groups of students can select another topic (e.g., tigers, hurricanes, molecules) and present information about it using the same structure. Patricia Grossman's *Very First Things to Know about Frogs* follows a number pattern. David Schwartz's *G Is for Googol: A Math Alphabet Book* follows an alphabet pattern.

Another method of literary borrowing is copy change or creative imitation (Leyson, 1989). Copy change does not require the use of predictable books. The teacher may use a selection from any book he or she believes models effective language. Students rewrite the passage, making specified changes. The rewriting possibilities are endless and include the following:

1. Change the setting.
2. Change the main character from a female to a male.
3. Change verbs from present tense to past tense.
4. Change from a third-person voice to a first-person voice.
5. Change all adjectives.

Student versions of the passage may be bound together in a class book and displayed.

Student books should be placed in a classroom library or in any location where they are visible and accessible. Class books are intended to be handled and read over and over again. Sharing need not be restricted to the immediate classroom. Students may read their books to students in other classrooms or take one home overnight and share it with family members.

Many student-created books contain a "reader-response" page. This page typically is placed at the end of the book and invites written comments from readers, including other students, classroom guests, the principal, parents, and siblings.

In the remainder of this chapter, we provide directions for constructing *pop-up books, accordion books, fold-up books, upside-down books, retelling picture books, graduated-pages books*, and *baggie books*.

The purposes of engaging children in bookmaking activities are as follows:

- To motivate students to read and write
- To prompt creative expression and extend understandings of text
- To promote problem solving and decision making
- To provide a means for sharing
- To promote language development
- To promote an understanding of reading and writing as personally meaningful, communicative acts

POP-UP BOOKS

Pop-up books are fun and easy to construct. Students enjoy the three-dimensional nature of these books. To make a pop-up book, follow these simple directions:

1. Fold a piece of paper in half. Construction paper provides the best thickness and support for the pop-up pictures, but copy paper will do. Make two cuts of equal length about one inch apart into the creased edge of the paper.

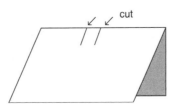

2. Open the paper so the two halves form a right angle. Pull the cut section through and fold it inward.

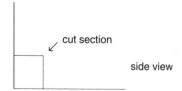

3. Paste a picture onto the cut section as shown.

You will probably want to have your students draw background pictures prior to pasting the pop-ups onto the page. The text also should be written on the paper prior to pasting and is typically on the bottom half of the paper.

Several pop-up figures may be placed on one page. Their sizes can vary by making shorter or longer cuts and by making the cuts closer together or farther apart. Each page should be constructed separately.

4. After each page is constructed, stack the folded pages in order, and glue them together.

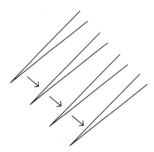

ACCORDION BOOKS

Accordion books provide an excellent opportunity for problem solving as students summarize a book. First, the students must divide a reading selection into meaningful sections. The number of sections will depend partly on the age of the students. If the students are working in groups, each student illustrates and writes text for one of the sections on a 9-by-12-inch piece of tagboard. The boards are then lined up end to end and taped or tied together in sequence. Books may stand freely on counters accordion-style or be folded for storage.

To ensure a cohesive product, group members should thoroughly discuss and agree on the text and illustrations prior to making individual assignments. If students do not discuss details, they run the risk of having a final product that lacks continuity and is clumsy. For example, one page may be written in the present tense and the next in the past tense, or the protagonist may be blond on one page and brunette on the next.

It is always interesting to have groups share their completed books. Students will notice that each group chose to summarize and illustrate the selection differently. Groups may vary in the events they chose to depict and in their illustrations.

Younger children may need to be guided through the summarization of the selection and the assignment of individual sections.

FOLD-UP BOOKS

Students can create a book that opens like a conventional book by folding and cutting a single sheet of paper. The size of the book will depend on the size of the paper used. Some students will enjoy making big books using butcher paper, and others will prefer to make miniatures using an 8½-by-11-inch piece of paper. Directions must be followed carefully.

1. Fold a rectangular piece of paper into eighths as shown, pressing firmly on the creases. Open the paper, then refold the opposite direction on the same folds, again creasing firmly.

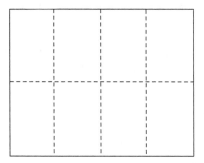

2. Fold the paper in half and cut on the center line as shown.

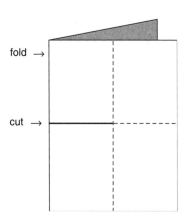

3. Open the paper. Lift points *a* and *c*, pulling them upward and away from each other so that points *b* and *d* come together. This will be difficult if folds are not well creased.

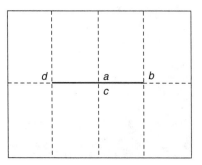

Your paper should look like this from the top:

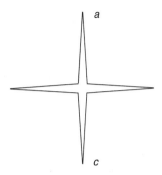

4. Bring all flaps together to form the book. Crease all folds.

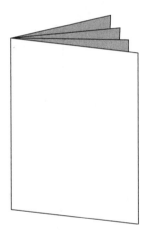

5. Students write and illustrate the pages of their book.

Fold-up books can be unfolded and photocopied to make a class set. Additionally, they can be unfolded, turned text side down, and refolded so a second book can be created on the same piece of paper.

UPSIDE-DOWN BOOKS

This type of book is useful when contrasting ideas are discussed or suggested by a piece of literature. One idea is written on one side of a piece of paper, and the contrasting idea is written upside down on the reverse side. For example, students may write contrasting information about the Earth's poles after reading *North Pole South Pole*, by Nancy Smiler Levinson. In the steps below, students write about both a terrible day and a wonderful day after reading *Alexander and the Terrible, Horrible, No Good, Very Bad Day*, by Judith Viorst.

1. Each student completes the prompt "It was a terrible, horrible, no good, very bad day when . . ." on a piece of paper and illustrates it.

2. Upside down and on the reverse side of the paper, each student completes and illustrates the second prompt "It was a wonderful, delightful, marvelous, fantastic day when. . . ." Students may complete the second picture and narration on a separate piece of paper. Papers may subsequently be pasted on a sheet of construction paper, one on the front and one upside down on the back.

3. All student papers are collected and stacked together, the same side up. In other words, all the "terrible day" sentences and illustrations are facing up, and all the "wonderful day" sentences and illustrations are facing down (and are upside down). An appropriate title page should be added to on the front and the back. Bind the pages with staples, ribbons, brads, or whatever is available. When the book is read in one direction, it describes very bad days. When the book is turned over and upside down, it describes wonderful days.

Information recorded in a contrast chart can provide ideas for an upside-down book. For example, the advantages and disadvantages of being two inches tall were listed in a contrast chart for *Stuart Little,* by E. B. White, in Chapter Two of this book. Students may create an upside-down book based on this chart with one side of the paper illustrating "A good thing about being two inches tall is . . ." and the reverse side of the paper illustrating "A bad thing about being two inches tall is . . . ."

RETELLING PICTURE BOOKS

Retelling picture books allow students to retell stories with the help of attached characters that can be moved on and off the pages of a book. First, settings are identified and illustrations are drawn, painted, or cut and pasted onto pieces of paper that become the pages of the book. A title page is created that includes a pocket in which characters may be stored. The pages are then bound together by any means.

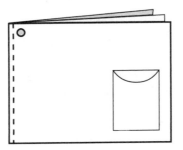

Next, characters are drawn onto tagboard and cut out. A hole is punched in each character, and a ribbon is tied through the hole. The other end of the ribbon is tied through a hole punched in the upper left-hand corner of the book. The ribbons must be long enough so that the students can move the characters freely. Three feet is a good length.

Students may then move the characters onto each page of the book as they retell the story.

One student teacher constructed a retelling picture book with a class of kindergarteners. She had each of her students make the following illustrations for *Goldilocks and the Three Bears*, by Lorinda Bryan Cauley, on 12-by-18-inch pieces of construction paper:

Page 1:   the bears' house in the middle of a forest

Page 2:   three bowls of porridge with the words *Papa, Mama,* and *Baby* written on them

Page 3:   three chairs and a stairway

Page 4:   three beds

After a title page was created and the pages were bound together, each student drew a picture of Goldilocks on tagboard and cut it out. Each also drew the three bears, cut them out, and pasted them together side by side so they could be moved about as a single entity. Goldilocks and the bears were then connected by ribbons to a corner of the book as just described.

When the children retold the story, they removed the characters from the pocket on the title page, opened the first page of the book, and moved the appropriate characters onto the page. On page 1, the bears were moved from the house into the forest to go for a walk. Goldilocks was moved onto the page to discover the bears' open house. On page 2, Goldilocks was moved from bowl to bowl before finding Baby Bear's porridge just right to eat. The students continued retelling the story while moving the characters from page to page.

A retelling picture book provides students with a structure for retelling a story, and the scenes serve as reminders for each part of the story. Retelling picture books are very motivational and promote language development. Retelling picture books are adaptable to many grade levels. Older students may make books for younger ones or may develop a retelling picture book for a section of a novel they are reading.

GRADUATED-PAGES BOOKS

Graduated-pages books are especially useful for making reference-type books because the pages are laid out so the reader can flip quickly to a topic of interest. The steps for making a graduated-pages book are as follows.

1. Decide on the number of pages in the book, including the title page. Divide the number of pages by two to determine the number of sheets of paper needed. For example, if you plan on an eight-page book, you will need four sheets of paper.

2. Set the papers in an overlapping stack, leaving one-half to one inch of each paper exposed.

3. Fold the stack of papers as shown. Staple at the folded edge, if desired.

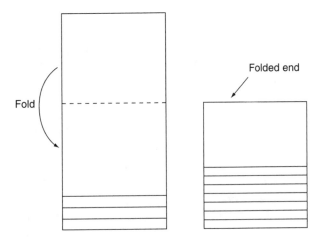

4. Students label each page at the exposed edge. This label provides the topic addressed on the page and allows readers to quickly find information.

After reading or listening to a book or several books about bats, students might write what they have learned in a graduated-pages book, labeling each page with a main idea and sharing drawings and details that can be viewed or read when the book is opened to the appropriate page. For example, one page might be labeled "Bats are mammals." Drawings and a discussion of the classification or physical characteristics of bats would be found on this page. Another page might be labeled "Bats use echolocation." A description of bats' use of echoes to locate food would be found on this page.

Books can be constructed either to open upwards, as shown in the diagrams above, or to open to the left like a more conventional book as shown here.

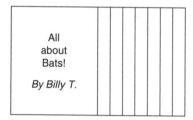

BAGGIE BOOKS

Baggie books are made with resealable plastic bags, cardstock, and tape. Pages of the book are created on cardstock and then inserted into baggies that are taped together at the sealed end. These books have several advantages. First, they are reusable because the cardstock pages can be removed from the baggies and replaced with new pages. Second, objects related to the writing can be slipped into the baggies. For example, if students write a book in response to *Flowers Fruits Seeds*, by Jerome Wexler, they can put various seeds in their baggies. Third, the baggie serves as a laminate to the cardstock pages, and students can write on the baggie with erasable markers, allowing opportunities for interaction with the content of the text.

Sandwich-size baggies are commonly used in making baggie books, but larger baggies work well too. After determining the baggie size, the teacher cuts cardstock so it fits comfortably into the baggie. Cardstock is preferable to paper because its stiffness makes it easier to slide into and out of the baggie. The steps for constructing baggie books are as follows:

1. Students write and illustrate the pages of their book, using the front and back sides of the cardstock.

2. Students tape baggies together. Each baggie will hold one piece of cardstock, or two pages of the book. Thus, four baggies will yield an eight-page book. Wide tape is most effective for taping the baggies together, and teachers often make colored tape available to their students. Some teachers suggest that the students staple the baggies before binding the pages of their book with tape. If the pages are stapled, holes result, which is a problem only if the students want to put a very fine material, such as sand, into their baggies. If the pages are only taped, the teacher will need to support young children to ensure that all the baggies make contact with the tape. To do this, the baggies should be laid on top of each other in a slightly staggered fashion as shown. Alternatively, baggies can be taped together two at a time. Then each pair is taped to another pair, and each set is taped to another set until all the baggies are taped together. This technique, however, requires more tape than the teacher may wish to use.

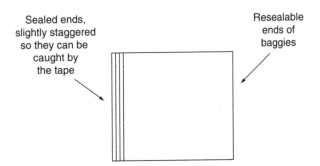

Sealed ends, slightly staggered so they can be caught by the tape

Resealable ends of baggies

3. Cardstock pages are inserted into the baggies, along with any objects the students choose to include.

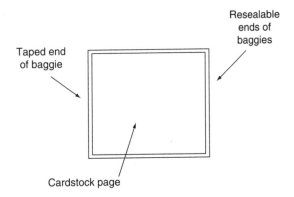

Resealable ends of baggies

Taped end of baggie

Cardstock page

CONCLUSION

Constructing their own books in response to literature is a highly motivational activity that promotes children's comprehension and language development. In addition, it reinforces a view of reading and writing as acts of communication. It is one of the most meaningful literacy activities in which students of any age can engage, and at the same time it can be supportive of other areas of the curriculum.

REFERENCES

Bonne, R. (1985). *I know an old lady.* New York: Scholastic.
Brown, A. (1975). Recognition, reconstruction, and recall of narrative sequences of preoperational children. *Child Development, 46,* 155–156.
Carle, E. (1987). *The Very Hungry Caterpillar.* New York: Scholastic.
Cauley, L. B. (1981). *Goldilocks and the three bears.* New York: Putnam.
Cutts, D. (1979). *The house that Jack built:* Mahwah, NJ: Troll Associates.
Grossman, P. (1999). *Very first things to know about frogs.* New York: Workman.
Koskinen, P., Gambrell, L., Kapinus, B., & Heathington, B. (1988). Retelling: A strategy for enhancing students' reading comprehension. *The Reading Teacher, 41,* 892–896.

Lancia, P.J. (1997). Literary borrowing: The effects of literature on children's writing. *The Reading Teacher, 50,* 470–475.

Langstaff, J. (1973). *Over in the meadow.* New York: Harcourt Brace Jovanovich.

Levinson, N.S. (2002). *North Pole South Pole.* New York: Holiday House.

Leyson, E. (1989). Authors teach literacy: Modeling, imitating, creating. In *From literacy to literature: Reading and writing for the language-minority student* (pp. 163–198). Los Angeles: Center for Academic Interinstitutional Programs, University of California.

Morrow, L. M. (1985). Retelling stories: A strategy for improving young children's comprehension, concept of story structure, and oral language complexity. *The Elementary School Journal, 85,* 647–661.

Petty, K. (1998). *I didn't know that crocodiles yawn to keep cool.* Brookfield, CT: Copper Beech.

Schwartz, D. M. (1998). *G is for googol: A math alphabet book.* Berkeley, CA: Tricycle.

Sendak, M. (1986). *Chicken soup with rice.* New York: Scholastic.

Southgate, V. (1966). *The little red hen.* Loughborough, England: Wills & Hepworth.

Viorst, J. (1976). *Alexander and the terrible, horrible, no good, very bad day.* New York: Macmillan.

Wexler, J. (1987). *Flowers fruits seeds.* New York: Simon & Schuster.

White, E.B. (1973). *Stuart Little.* New York: Harper & Row.

Afterword

We hope that teachers will find the activities described in this book useful for promoting meaningful interactions with literature and inspiring a love of reading in their students. Before teachers incorporate these activities into their literature programs, however, we would like to issue a few cautions.

First, it is important that teachers know their students and make instructional decisions based on students' interests and needs. Activities that are appropriate for some groups of students may be less valuable for others. For example, some students may have considerable background knowledge on a particular topic and so will need less time devoted to building background knowledge prior to interacting with the selection. Other students may have little background knowledge on the topic and will profit from participation in a number of prereading activities. Likewise, reluctant readers will benefit from activities that spark their interest and establish connections between their lives and the literature.

Second, teachers should not be surprised if students do not engage in a grand conversation the first time an activity is attempted. Many children have experienced only gentle (or not so gentle!) inquisitions in school settings. They have learned that there is only one correct answer, that the most verbal students will provide it, or that if they wait long enough the teacher will provide it. This is especially true of older students who have had more time to learn these lessons. Given these expectations, it is not likely that all students will respond enthusiastically to the activities at first. Teachers may need to attempt the activities several times before achieving participation from everyone, while at the same time building trust and new expectations in their students.

Third, these activities should not be used as worksheets that are to be completed independently and collected for a grade. They are intended to arouse curiosity, spark conversation, activate background knowledge, focus attention on themes or language, promote comprehension, encourage reflection on issues or events encountered in books, and help students find literature selections personally meaningful. Few independently completed worksheets achieve these goals. They can be achieved, however, through meaningful interaction among students and with the teacher.

Fourth, literature activities should not be overused. We know one teacher who implemented several prereading activities before every chapter of a novel. We were not surprised when she told us that her students disliked the novel and lost enthusiasm for the activities. Anything can be overdone. Teachers should exercise reason when using literature activities before, during, and after reading. Sometimes it is most appropriate to use none at all.

Finally, teachers should provide students with many opportunities to read and listen to literature in the classroom throughout the day and in many contexts. These opportunities, along with an extensive classroom library, will go a long way toward promoting a love of reading.

APPENDIX A

Internet Resources

SELECTED AUTHOR WEBSITES

www.almaada.com (Alma Flor Ada)
www.avi-writer.com (Avi)
www.ayles.com (Jim Aylesworth)
www.bernardmost.com (Bernard Most)
www.betsybyars.com (Betsy Byars)
www.eric-carle.com (Eric Carle)
www.ezra-jack-keats.org (Ezra Jack Keats)
www.janbrett.com (Jan Brett)
www.jeancraigheadgeorge.com (Jean Craighead George)
www.judyblum.com (Judy Blum)
www.loislowry.com (Lois Lowry)
www.patriciapolacco.com (Patricia Polacco)
www.sharoncreech.com (Sharon Creech)
www.terabithia.com (Katherine Paterson)
www.willhobbsauthor.com (Will Hobbs)

LISTS OF AWARD-WINNING CHILDREN'S LITERATURE

www.ala.org/ala/alsc/awardsscholarships/childrensnotable/notablec booklist/currentnotable.htm
Provides a list of books selected by the Association for Library Service to Children as the best in children's literature

www.ala.org/alsc/belpre.html
Provides information about the Pura Belpré Award for Latino/a authors and illustrators for books best portraying the Latino/a cultural experience and a list of award winners

www.ala.org/alsc/caldecott.html
Provides information about the Caldecott Medal for the illustrator of the most distinguished picture book and a list of award winners

www.ala.org/alsc/newbery.html
Provides information about the Newbery Medal for distinguished children's literature and a list of award winners

www.ala.org/ala/pr2004/prfeb2004/SchneiderFamilyBookAw.htm
Provides information about the Schneider Family book award for books depicting the disability experience and list of award winners

www.ala.org/srrt/csking/
Provides information about the Coretta Scott King Award for illustrators and authors of African descent whose books promote an understanding and appreciation of the American Dream and a list of award winners

www.cde.ca.gov/ci/sc/ll/
Provides a list of outstanding science- and mathematics-related literature for children and adolescents

www.dawcl.com
Provides a database of award-winning children's literature

www.ncte.org/about/awards/sect/elem/106877.htm
Provides information about the Orbis Pictus Nonfiction Award and a list of award winners

www.nsta.org/pubs/sc/ostblist.asp
Provides a list of Outstanding Science Trade Books for Children

www.reading.org/resources/tools/choices_childrens.html
Provides a list of books selected by children as favorites

www.reading.org/resources/tools/choices_teachers.html
Provides a list of books for children selected by teachers, reading specialists, and librarians

www.reading.org/resources/tools/choices_young_adults.html
Provides a list of books selected by adolescents as favorites

www.socialstudies.org/resources/notable/
Provides a list of notable trade books in the social studies

OTHER WEBSITES OF INTEREST

www.bibliofind.com
Locates out-of-print, hard-to-find, and rare books

www.bookfinder.com
Locates new and used books

www.acs.ucalgary.ca/~dkbrown/index.html
Provides information about Internet resources related to books for children and adults

www.cbcbooks.org
Provides information about the Children's Book Council which, among other activities, sponsors Young People's Poetry Week and Children's Book Week

www.hbook.com
Provides information about books for children and young adults

www.poets.org
The website of the Academy of American Poets whose mission it is to foster the appreciation of contemporary poetry

www.readwritethink.org/
Provides lesson plans and related materials for language arts teachers

APPENDIX B

Award-Winning Literature

CALDECOTT MEDAL

The Caldecott Medal, first awarded in 1938, is presented annually to the illustrator of the most distinguished picture book published in the United States. The award is named after Randolph Caldecott, a British illustrator, and is given by the Children's Services Division of the American Library Association.

1938 *Animals of the Bible* by Helen Dean Fish, ill. by Dorothy P. Lathrop (Frederick A. Stokes)

1939 *Mei Li* by Thomas Handforth (Doubleday, Doran)

1940 *Abraham Lincoln* by Ingri and Edgar Parin D'Aulaire (Doubleday, Doran)

1941 *They Were Strong and Good* by Robert Lawson (Viking)

1942 *Make Way for Ducklings* by Robert McCloskey (Viking)

1943 *The Little House* by Virginia Lee Burton (Houghton Mifflin)

1944 *Many Moons* by James Thurber, ill. by Louis Slobodkin (Harcourt Brace)

1945 *Prayer for a Child* by Rachel Field, ill. by Elizabeth Orton Jones (Macmillan)

1946 *The Rooster Crows* (traditional Mother Goose), ill. by Maud and Miska Petersham (Macmillan)

1947 *The Little Island* by Golden MacDonald, ill. by Leonard Weisgard (Doubleday)

1948 *White Snow, Bright Snow* by Alvin Tresselt, ill. by Roger Duvoisin (Lothrop, Lee & Shepard)

1949 *The Big Snow* by Betta and Elmer Hader (Macmillian)

1950 *Song of the Swallows* by Leo Politi (Charles Scribner's Sons)

1951 *The Egg Tree* by Katherine Milhous (Charles Scribner's Sons)

1952 *Finders Keepers* by William Lipkind, ill. by Nicholas Mordvinoff (Harcourt)

1953 *The Biggest Bear* by Lynd Ward (Houghton Mifflin)

1954 *Madeline's Rescue* by Ludwig Bemelmans (Viking)

1955 *Cinderella, or the Little Glass Slipper* by Charles Perrault, trans. and ill. by Marcia Brown (Charles Scribner's Sons)

1956 *Frog Went A-Courtin'* by John Langstaff, ill. by Feodor Rojankovsky (Harcourt)

1957 *A Tree is Nice* by Janice May Udry, ill. by Marc Simont (Harper and Brothers)

1958 *Time of Wonder* by Robert McCloskey (Viking)

1959 *Chanticleer and the Fox* (adapted from Chaucer) by Barbara Cooney (Thomas Y. Crowell)

1960 *Nine Days to Christmas* by Marie Hall Ets and Aurora Labastida, ill. by Marie Hall Ets (Viking)

1961 *Baboushka and the Three Kings* by Ruth Robbins, ill. by Nicolas Sidjakov (Parnassus Imprints)

1962 *Once a Mouse . . .* by Marcia Brown (Charles Scribner's Sons)

1963 *The Snowy Day* by Ezra Jack Keats (Viking)

1964 *Where the Wild Things Are* by Maurice Sendak (Harper & Row)

1965 *May I Bring a Friend?* by Beatrice Schenk de Regniers, ill. by Beni Monstresor (Atheneum)

1966 *Always Room for One More* by Sorche Nic Leodhas, ill. by Nonny Hogrogian (Holt, Rinehart, & Winston)

1967 *Sam, Bangs & Moonshine* by Evaline Ness (Holt, Rinehart, & Winston)

1968 *Drummer Hoff* by Barbara Emberley, ill. by Ed Emberley (Prentice-Hall)

1969 *The Fool of the World and the Flying Ship* by Arthur Ransom, ill. by Uri Shulevitz (Farrar, Straus & Giroux)

1970 *Sylvester and the Magic Pebble* by William Steig (Windmill/Simon & Schuster)

1971 *A Story, A Story* by Gail E. Haley (Atheneum)

1972 *One Fine Day* by Nonny Hogrogian (Macmillan)

1973 *The Funny Little Woman* by Arlene Mosel, ill. by Blair Lent (E. P. Dutton)

1974 *Duffy and the Devil* by Harve Zemach, ill. by Margot Zemach (Farrar, Straus & Giroux)

1975 *Arrow to the Sun* by Gerald McDermott (Viking)

1976 *Why Mosquitoes Buzz in People's Ears* by Verna Aardema, ill. by Leo and Diane Dillon (Dial)

1977 *Ashanti to Zulu: African Traditions* by Margaret Musgrove, ill. by Leo and Diane Dillon (Dial)

1978 *Noah's Ark* by Peter Spier (Doubleday)

1979 *The Girl Who Loved Wild Horses* by Paul Goble (Bradbury)

1980 *Ox-Cart Man* by Donald Hall, ill. by Barbara Cooney (Viking)

1981 *Fables* by Arnold Lobel (Harper & Row)

1982 *Jumanji* by Chris Van Allsburg (Houghton Mifflin)

1983 *Shadow* by Blaise Cendrars, ill. by Marcia Brown (Charles Scribner's Sons)

1984 *The Glorious Flight: Across the Channel with Louis Bleriot, July 25, 1909* by Alice and Martin Provensen (Viking)

1985 *St. George and the Dragon* by Margaret Hodges, ill. by Trina Schart Hyman (Little, Brown)

1986 *The Polar Express* by Chris Van Allsburg (Houghton Mifflin)

1987 *Hey, Al* by Arthur Yorinks, ill. by Richard Egielski (Farrar, Straus & Giroux)

1988 *Owl Moon* by Jane Yolen, ill. by John Schoenherr (Philomel)

1989 *Song and Dance Man* by Karen Ackerman, ill. by Stephen Gammell (Alfred A. Knopf)

1990 *Lon Po Po: A Red Riding Hood Story from China* by Ed Young (Philomel)
1991 *Black and White* by Davis Macaulay (Houghton Mifflin)
1992 *Tuesday* by David Weisner (Clarion)
1993 *Mirette on the High Wire* by Emily Arnold McCully (G. P. Putnam's Sons)
1994 *Grandfather's Journey* by Allen Say (Houghton Mifflin)
1995 *Smokey Night* by Eve Bunting, ill. by David Diaz (Harcourt Brace)
1996 *Officer Buckle and Gloria* by Peggy Rathmann (Putnam)
1997 *Golem* by David Wisniewski (Clarion)
1998 *Rapunzel* by Paul O. Zelinksy (E. P. Dutton)
1999 *Snowflake Bentley* by Jaqueline Briggs Martin, ill. by Mary Azarian (Houghton Mifflin)
2000 *Joseph Had a Little Overcoat* by Simms Taback (Viking)
2001 *So You Want to Be President?* By Judith St. George, ill. by David Small (Philomel)
2002 *The Three Pigs* by David Wiesner (Clarion/Houghton Mifflin)
2003 *My Friend Rabbit* by Eric Rohmann (Roaring Brook/Millbrook)
2004 *The Man Who Walked Between the Towers* by Mordicai Gerstein (Roaring Brook/Millbrook)
2005 *Kitten's First Full Moon* by Kevin Henkes (Greenwillow)
2006 _____
2007 _____
2008 _____
2009 _____
2010 _____

NEWBERY MEDAL

The Newbery Medal, first presented in 1922, is given annually for the most distinguished contribution to children's literature published in the United States. The award is named after John Newbery, the first English publisher of books for children, and is given by the Children's Services Division of the American Library Association.

1922 *The Story of Mankind* by Hendrik Willem van Loon (Boni & Liveright)
1923 *The Voyages of Doctor Dolittle* by Hugh Lofting (Frederick A. Stokes)
1924 *The Dark Frigate* by Charles Hawes (Atlantic Monthly Press)
1925 *Tales from Silver Lands* by Charles Finger (Doubleday, Page)
1926 *Shen of the Sea* by Arthur Bowie Chrisman (E. P. Dutton)
1927 *Smoky, the Cowhorse* by Will James (Charles Scribner's Sons)
1928 *Gayneck, the Story of a Pigeon* by Dhan Gopal Mukerji (E. P. Dutton)
1929 *The Trumpeter of Krakow* by Eric P. Kelly (Macmillan)
1930 *Hitty, Her First Hundred Years* by Rachel Field (Macmillan)
1931 *The Cat Who Went to Heaven* by Elizabeth Coatsworth (Macmillan)
1932 *Waterless Mountain* by Laura Adams Armer (Longmans, Green)
1933 *Young Fu of the Upper Yangtze* by Elizabeth Foreman Lewis (John C. Winston)
1934 *Invincible Louisa: The Story of the Author of Little Women* by Cornelia Meigs (Little, Brown)
1935 *Dobry* by Monica Shannon (Viking)
1936 *Caddie Woodlawn* by Carol Ryrie Brink (Macmillan)

1937 *Roller Skates* by Ruth Sawyer (Viking)
1938 *The White Stag* by Kate Seredy (Viking)
1939 *Thimble Summer* by Elizabeth Enright (Rinehart)
1940 *Daniel Boone* by James Daugherty (Viking)
1941 *Call It Courage* by Armstrong Sperry (Macmillan)
1942 *The Matchlock Gun* by Walter D. Edmonds (Dodd, Mead)
1943 *Adam of the Road* by Elizabeth Janet Gray (Viking)
1944 *Johnny Tremain* by Esther Forbes (Houghton Mifflin)
1945 *Rabbit Hill* by Robert Lawson (Viking)
1946 *Strawberry Girl* by Lois Lenski (J. B. Lippincott)
1947 *Miss Hickory* by Carolyn Sherwin Bailey (Viking)
1948 *The Twenty-One Balloons* by William Pene du Bois (Viking)
1949 *King of the Wind* by Marguerite Henry (Rand McNally)
1950 *The Door in the Wall* by Marguerite de Angeli (Doubleday)
1951 *Amos Fortune, Free Man* by Elizabeth Yates (E. P. Dutton)
1952 *Ginger Pye* by Eleanor Estes (Harcourt, Brace)
1953 *Secret of the Andes* by Ann Nolan Clark (Viking)
1954 *. . . and now Miguel* by Joseph Krumgold (Thomas Y. Crowell)
1955 *The Wheel on the School* by Meindert DeJong (Harper)
1956 *Carry On, Mr. Bowditch* by Jean Lee Latham (Houghton Mifflin)
1957 *Miracles on Maple Hill* by Virginia Sorensen (Harcourt Brace)
1958 *Rifles for Watie* by Harold Keith (Thomas Y. Crowell)
1959 *The Witch of Blackbird Pond* by Elizabeth George Speare (Houghton Mifflin)
1960 *Onion John* by Joseph Krumgold (Thomas Y. Crowell)
1961 *Island of the Blue Dolphins* by Scott O'Dell (Houghton Mifflin)
1962 *The Bronze Bow* by Elizabeth George Speare (Houghton Mifflin)
1963 *A Wrinkle in Time* by Madeleine L'Engle (Farrar, Straus)
1964 *It's Like This, Cat* by Emily Cheney Neville (Harper & Row)
1965 *Shadow of a Bull* by Maia Wojciechowska (Atheneum)
1966 *I, Juan de Pareja* by Elizabeth Borten de Trevino (Farrar, Straus & Giroux)
1967 *Up a Road Slowly* by Irene Hunt (Follett)
1968 *From the Mixed-Up Files of Mrs. Basil E. Frankweiler* by E. L. Konigsburg (Atheneum)
1969 *The High King* by Lloyd Alexander (Holt, Rinehart, & Winston)
1970 *Sounder* by William H. Armstrong (Harper & Row)
1971 *Summer of the Swans* by Betsy Byars (Viking)
1972 *Mrs. Frisby and the Rats of NIMH* by Robert C. O'Brien (Atheneum)
1973 *Julie of the Wolves* by Jean Craighead George (Harper & Row)
1974 *The Slave Dancer* by Paula Fox (Bradbury)
1975 *M. C. Higgins, the Great* by Virginia Hamilton (Macmillan)
1976 *The Grey King* by Susan Cooper (Atheneum)
1977 *Roll of Thunder, Hear My Cry* by Mildred D. Taylor (Dial)
1978 *Bridge to Terabithia* by Katherine Paterson (Thomas Y. Crowell)
1979 *The Westing Game* by Ellen Raskin (E. P. Dutton)
1980 *A Gathering of Days: A New England Girl's Journal 1830–32* by Joan Blos (Charles Scribner's Sons)
1981 *Jacob Have I Loved* by Katherine Paterson (Thomas Y. Crowell)
1982 *A Visit to William Blake's Inn: Poems for Innocent and Experienced Travelers* by Nancy Willard (Harcourt Brace Jovanovich)
1983 *Dicey's Song* by Cynthia Voigt (Atheneum)
1984 *Dear Mr. Henshaw* by Beverly Clearly (Morrow)

1985 *The Hero and the Crown* by Robin McKinley (Greenwillow)
1986 *Sarah, Plain and Tall* by Patricia MacLachlan (Harper & Row)
1987 *The Whipping Boy* by Sid Fleischman (Greenwillow)
1988 *Lincoln: A Photobiography* by Russell Freedman (Clarion)
1989 *Joyful Noise: Poems for Two Voices* by Paul Fleischman (Harper & Row)
1990 *Number the Stars* by Lois Lowry (Houghton Mifflin)
1991 *Maniac Magee* by Jerry Spinelli (Little, Brown)
1992 *Shiloh* by Phyllis Reynolds Naylor (Atheneum)
1993 *Missing May* by Cynthia Rylant (Orchard)
1994 *The Giver* by Lois Lowry (Houghton Mifflin)
1995 *Walk Two Moons* by Sharon Creech (HarperCollins)
1996 *The Midwife's Apprentice* by Karen Cushman (Clarion)
1997 *The View from Saturday* by E. L. Konigsburg (Atheneum)
1998 *Out of the Dust* by Karen Hesse (Scholastic)
1999 *Holes* by Louis Sachar (Farrar, Straus & Giroux)
2000 *Bud, Not Buddy* by Christopher Paul Curtis (Delacorte)
2001 *A Year Down Yonder* by Richard Peck (Dial)
2002 *A Single Shard* by Linda Sue Park (Clarion/Houghton Mifflin)
2003 *Crispin: The Cross of Lead* by Avi (Hyperion)
2004 *The Tale of Despereaux: Being the Story of a Mouse, a Princess, Some Soup, and a Spool of Thread* by Kate DiCamillo (Candlewick)
2005 *Kira-Kira* by Cynthia Kadohata (Atheneum)
2006 _____
2007 _____
2008 _____
2009 _____
2010 _____

ORBIS PICTUS AWARD

The Orbis Pictus Award for Outstanding Nonfiction for Children, established by the National Council of Teachers of English in 1989, recognizes excellence in nonfiction writing for children. The name commemorates a 1657 publication, *Orbis Pictus—The World in Pictures*, by Johannes Amos Comenius, believed to be the first book actually planned for children.

1990 *The Great Little Madison* by Jean Fritz (Putnam)
1991 *Franklin Delano Roosevelt* by Russell Freedman (Clarion)
1992 *Flight: The Journey of Charles Lindbergh* by Robert Burleigh and Mike Wimmer (Philomel)
1993 *Children of the Dust Bowl: The True Story of the School at Weedpatch Camp* by Jerry Stanley (Crown)
1994 *Across America on an Emigrant Train* by Jim Murphy (Clarion)
1995 *Safari beneath the Sea: The Wonder of the North Pacific Coast* by Diane Swanson (Sierra Club)
1996 *The Great Fire* by Jim Murphy (Scholastic)
1997 *Leonardo da Vinci* by Diane Stanley (Morrow)
1998 *An Extraordinary Life: The Story of a Monarch Butterfly* by Laurence Pringle (Orchard)
1999 *Shipwreck at the Bottom of the World: The Extraordinary True Story of Shackleton and the Endurance* by Jennifer Armstrong (Crown)

2000 *Through My Eyes* by Ruby Bridges and Margo Lundell (Scholastic)
2001 *Hurry Freedom: African Americans in Gold Rush California* by Jerry Stanley (Crown)
2002 *Black Potatoes: The Story of the Great Irish Famine, 1845–1850* by Susan Campbell Bartoletti (Houghton Mifflin)
2003 *When Marian Sang: The True Recital of Marian Anderson: The Voice of a Century* by Pam Munoz Ryan (Scholastic)
2004 *An American Plague: The True and Terrifying Story of the Yellow Fever Epidemic of 1793* by Jim Murphy (Clarion)
2005 *York's Adventures with Lewis and Clark: An African-American's Part in the Great Expansion* by Rhoda Blumberg (HarperCollins)
2006 _____
2007 _____
2008 _____
2009 _____
2010 _____

CORETTA SCOTT KING AWARD

The Coretta Scott King Awards are presented annually by the Coretta Scott King Task Force of the American Library Association's Ethnic Multicultural Information Exchange Round Table. Awardees are illustrators and authors of African descent whose books promote an understanding and appreciation of the American Dream. The awards commemorate Dr. Martin Luther King, Jr., and honor Coretta Scott King.

Illustrator Awards

1974 *Ray Charles* by Sharon Bell Mathis, ill. by George Ford (Crowell)
1975 No award
1976 No award
1977 No award
1978 *Africa Dream* by Eloise Greenfield, ill. by Carole Bayard (Crowell)
1979 *Something on My Mind* by Nikki Grimes, ill. by Tom Feelings (Dial)
1980 *Cornrows* by Camille Yarborough, ill. by Carole Bayard (Coward-McCann)
1981 *Beat the Story Drum, Pum-Pum* by Ashley Bryan (Atheneum)
1982 *Mother Crocodile: An Uncle Amadou Tale from Senegal* by Rosa Guy, ill. by John Steptoe (Delacorte)
1983 *Black Child* by Peter Mugabane (Knopf)
1984 *My Mama Needs Me* by Mildred Pitts Walter, ill. by Pat Cummings (Lothrop)
1985 No award
1986 *The Patchwork Quilt* by Valerie Flournoy, ill. by Jerry Pinkney (Dial)
1987 *Half a Moon and One Whole Star* by Crescent Dragonwagon, ill. by Jerry Pinkney (Macmillan)
1988 *Mufaro's Beautiful Daughter: An African Tale* by John Steptoe (Lothrop)
1989 *Mirandy and Brother Wind* by Patricia McKissack, ill. by Jerry Pinkney (Knopf)
1990 *Nathaniel Talking* by Eloise Greenfield, ill. by Jan Spivey Guilerist (Black Butterfly)

1991 *Aida* by Leontyne Price, ill. by Leo and Diane Dillon (Harcourt)

1992 *Tar Beach* by Faith Ringgold (Crown)

1993 *The Origin of Life on Earth: An African Creation Myth* retold by David A. Anderson/SANKOFA, ill. by Kathleen Atkins Wilson (Sights)

1994 *Soul Looks Back in Wonder* by Phyllis Fogelman, ill. by Tom Feelings (Dial)

1995 *The Creation* by James Weldon Johnson, ill. by James Ransome (Holiday House)

1996 *The Middle Passage: White Ships Black Cargo* by Tom Feelings (Dial)

1997 *Minty: A Story of Young Harriet Tubman* by Alan Schroeder, ill. by Jerry Pinkney (Dial Books for Young Readers)

1998 *In Daddy's Arms I am Tall: African Americans Celebrating Fathers* by Alan Schroeder, ill. by Javaka Steptoe (Lee & Low)

1999 *i see the rhythm* by Toyomi Igus, ill. by Michele Wood (Children's Book Press)

2000 *In the Time of the Drums* by Kim L. Siegelson, ill. by Brian Pinkney (Hyperion)

2001 *Uptown* by Bryan Collier (Henry Holt)

2002 *Goin' Someplace Special* by Patricia McKissack, ill. by Jerry Pinkney (Anne Schwartz/Atheneum)

2003 *Talkin' About Bessie: The Story of Aviator Elizabeth Coleman* by Nikki Grimes, ill. by E.B. Lewis (Orchard/Scholastic)

2004 *Beautiful Blackbird* by Ashley Bryan (Atheneum)

2005 *Ellington Was Not a Street* by Ntozake Shange, ill. by Kadir Nelson (Simon & Schuster)

2006 _____

2007 _____

2008 _____

2009 _____

2010 _____

Author Award

1970 *Martin Luther King, Jr.: Man of Peace* by Lillie Patterson (Garrard)

1971 *Black Troubador: Langston Hughes* by Charlemae Rollins (Rand McNally)

1972 *17 Black Artists* by Elton C. Fax (Dodd)

1973 *I Never Had It Made: The Autobiography of Jackie Robinson* as told to Alfred Dickett (Putnam)

1974 *Ray Charles* by Sharon Bell Mathis (Crowell)

1975 *The Legend of Africana* by Dorothy Robinson (Johnson)

1976 *Duey's Tale* by Pearl Bailey (Harcourt)

1977 *The Story of Stevie Wonder* by James Haskins (Lothrop)

1978 *Africa Dream* by Eloise Greenfield (Crowell)

1979 *Escape to Freedom* by Ossie Davis (Viking)

1980 *The Young Landlords* by Walter Bean Myers (Viking)

1981 *This Life* by Sidney Poitier (Knopf)

1982 *Let the Circle Be Unbroken* by Mildred D. Taylor (Dial)

1983 *Sweet Whispers, Brother Rush* by Virginia Hamilton (Philomel)

1984 *Everett Anderson's Good-bye* by Lucille Clifton (Holt)

1985 *Motown and Didi* by Walter Dean Myers (Viking)

1986 *The People Could Fly: American Black Folktales* by Virginia Hamilton (Knopf)

1987 *Justin and the Best Biscuits in the World* by Mildred Pitts Walter (Lothrop)

1988 *The Friendship* by Mildred L. Taylor (Dial)

1989 *Fallen Angels* by Walter Dean Myers (Scholastic)

1990 *A Long Hard Journey: The Story of the Pullman Porter* by Patricia C. & Frederick L. McKissack (Walker)

1991 *The Road to Memphis* by Mildred D. Taylor (Dial)

1992 *Now is Your Time: The African American Struggle for Freedom* by Walter Dean Myers (HarperCollins)

1993 *Dark Thirty: Southern Tales of the Supernatural* by Patricia A. McKissack (Knopf)

1994 *Toning the Sweep* by Angela Johnson (Orchard)

1995 *Christmas in the Big House, Christmas in the Quarters* by Patricia C. & Frederick L. McKissack (Scholastic)

1996 *Her Stories* by Virginia Hamilton (Scholastic/Blue Sky)

1997 *Slam* by Walter Dean Myers (Scholastic)

1998 *Forged by Fire* by Sharon M. Draper (Atheneum)

1999 *Heaven* by Angela Johnson (Simon & Schuster)

2000 *Bud, Not Buddy* by Christopher Paul Curtis (Delacorte)

2001 *Miracle's Boys* by Jacqueline Woodson (G. P. Putman's Sons)

2002 *The Land* by Mildred Taylor (Phyllis Fogelman/Penguin Putnam)

2003 *Bronx Masquerade* by Nikki Grimes (Dial)

2004 *The First Part Last* by Angela Johnson (Simon & Schuster)

2005 *Remember: The Journey to School Integration* by Toni Morrison (Houghton Mifflin)

2006 _____

2007 _____

2008 _____

2009 _____

2010 _____

PURA BELPRÉ MEDAL

The Pura Belpré Award is presented to a Latino/Latina writer and illustrator whose work best portrays, affirms, and celebrates the Latino cultural experience. The award was established in 1996 and is cosponsored by the Association for Library Service to Children, a division of the American Library Association, and the National Association to Promote Library and Information Services to Latinos and the Spanish-Speaking.

Author

1996 *An Island Like You: Stories of the Barrio* by Judith Ortiz Cofer (Orchard)

1998 *Parrot in the Oven: mi vida* by Victor Martinez (HarperCollins)

2000 *Under the Royal Palms: A Childhood in Cuba* by Alma Flor Ada (Atheneum)

2002 *Esperanza Rising* by Pam Munoz Ryan (Scholastic)

2004 *Before We Were Free* by Julia Alvarez (Alfred A. Knopf)

2006 _____

2008 _____

2010 _____

Illustrator

1996 *Chato's Kitchen* by Gary Soto, ill. by Susan Guevara (Putnam)
1998 *Snapshots from the Wedding* by Gary Soto, ill. by Stephanie Garcia (Putnam)
2000 *Magic Windows* by Carmen Lomas Garza (Children's Book Press)
2002 *Chato and the Party Animals* by Gary Soto, ill. by Susan Guevara (Scholastic)
2004 *Just a Minute: A Trickster Tale and Counting Book* by Yuyi Morales (Chronicle)
2006 _____
2008 _____
2010 _____

SCHNEIDER FAMILY BOOK AWARD

The Schneider Family Book Award is given by the American Library Association to the author or illustrator of a book that embodies an artistic expression of the disability experience. The first awards were given in 2004.

Birth through Grade School Category

2004 *Looking Out for Sarah* by Glenna Lang (Charlesbridge)
2005 *My Pal, Victor/Mi Amigo, Victor* by Diane Gonzales Bertrand, ill. by Robert L. Sweetland (Raven Tree)
2006 _____
2007 _____
2008 _____
2009 _____
2010 _____

Middle School Category

2004 *A Mango-Shaped Space* by Wendy Mass (Little, Brown)
2005 *Becoming Naomi León* by Pam Muñoz Ryan (Scholastic)
2006 _____
2007 _____
2008 _____
2009 _____
2010 _____

Teen Category

2004 *Things Not Seen* by Andrew Clements (Philomel)
2005 *My Thirteenth Winter: A Memoir* by Samantha Abeel (Orchard)
2006 _____
2007 _____
2008 _____
2009 _____
2010 _____

Index